How the Bible Changes Lives

Joe R. Eagleman, PhD

CONTENTS

Chapter 1 – A Book Unlike Any Other

For thousands of years, countless volumes have been written, read, and forgotten, but the Bible remains unlike any other book in history. Composed over a span of roughly 1,500 years by more than forty authors from vastly different backgrounds—shepherds, kings, fishermen, prophets, and scholars—it carries a single, unified message of God's love and redemption. While most books are bound to a single culture, era, or worldview, the Bible has crossed continents, languages, and generations, shaping civilizations and touching lives from remote villages to bustling cities. Its words have been whispered in prison cells, read aloud in royal courts, smuggled across borders, and treasured in humble homes.

The Bible is not merely an ancient text; it is a living book that speaks directly to the human heart. Many have described opening its pages and feeling as if God Himself was speaking to them. Consider the story of John Newton, an eighteenth-century slave trader whose heart was as hard as the chains he used to bind others.

After encountering the Bible and wrestling with its message, Newton surrendered his life to Christ and later became a passionate advocate for the abolition of slavery. His transformation inspired one of the most beloved hymns in history—*Amazing Grace*. The book that once seemed irrelevant to him became the very foundation of his new life.

In modern times, the Bible's influence is just as powerful. Maria, a young woman in South America, grew up in an abusive household, convinced she had no value. One day, a neighbor invited her to a small Bible study. As she read Psalm 139—*"I am fearfully and wonderfully made"*—the words struck her like a beam of light in the darkness. She began to see herself as God saw her, not as the broken, unwanted child she believed she was. This newfound truth gave her courage to pursue education, help other women escape abusive situations, and raise her children in a home filled with love rather than fear.

The Bible changes lives not because of mere words on paper, but because its Author is alive. Its message doesn't fade with time or become outdated with shifting cultures. Whether in the heart of a hardened skeptic or the depths of someone feeling invisible and forgotten, the Bible has a way of reaching in, confronting lies, and planting seeds of truth that grow into transformed lives. It is indeed a book unlike any other—not simply to be read, but to be experienced.

Chapter 2 – The Living Word

Many books inspire, some even endure for generations, but the Bible is different—it is alive. This is not merely a poetic idea; it is a truth rooted in Scripture itself. Hebrews 4:12 declares, *"For the word of God is living and active, sharper than any two-edged sword."* Unlike static literature, the Bible has the remarkable ability to speak freshly into new situations, offering wisdom, correction, comfort, and guidance precisely when they are needed. A verse read years ago can suddenly take on new meaning when life circumstances change, as if the Author is tailoring His message personally for the reader.

Consider the story of a man named Sam, a corporate executive in New York City. For decades, he treated the Bible as a relic—respectable, but irrelevant. During a health crisis, his life came to a screeching halt. While in the hospital, a friend left a Bible on his bedside table. One sleepless night, he opened it at random to the Gospel of John. The words *"I am the way and the truth and the life"* seemed to leap off the page. He had read those words before, but now they penetrated his heart. Over the following weeks, as he read more, it felt as though the

Bible was holding a conversation with him—answering doubts, calming fears, and pointing him toward a relationship with Christ. The same words that had once seemed flat now breathed life into his weary soul.

This living quality of Scripture is not confined to moments of crisis; it can meet people in the ordinary rhythms of life. In rural Kenya, a young teacher named Esther read the Bible each morning before school. One day, while reading Matthew 5 about loving your enemies, she felt convicted about her hostility toward a rival teacher who had spread lies about her. That morning, the words seemed as though they had been written just for her situation. She chose to respond with kindness instead of retaliation. Over time, her unexpected grace softened her colleague's heart, and they became friends. Esther's obedience to a living word rippled outward, changing not just her heart but the atmosphere of the entire school.

The Bible is alive because its Author is alive. The Holy Spirit takes the words penned centuries ago and applies them directly to our present realities. A passage can comfort a grieving mother, convict a dishonest businessman, inspire a discouraged pastor, or challenge a complacent believer—all at the same time. It is as if the same eternal message is woven into countless personalized letters, each perfectly timed. This is the miracle of the living Word: it doesn't merely inform the mind; it transforms the heart in real time.

Chapter 3 – From Guilt to Grace

Guilt can be a heavy chain. It shackles the mind, steals peace, and whispers that past mistakes are too great to be forgiven. For many, guilt lingers for years, long after the offense is over, replaying scenes of failure in the quiet moments of the night. It drives some into isolation and others into self-destructive behaviors, as if punishing themselves could erase the wrongs. The Bible speaks directly to this deep human wound, not by pretending sin isn't real, but by offering a far greater truth: *grace*.

Grace is not earned, bargained for, or deserved—it is the free and undeserved favor of God. Through Scripture, God reaches into the darkest corners of a person's past and declares that forgiveness is possible, no matter how deep the stain. This is not a shallow, sentimental reassurance; it is grounded in the reality of Christ's sacrifice. *"There is now no condemnation for those who are in Christ Jesus"* (Romans 8:1) is not just a verse to memorize—it is a verdict that changes the entire identity of a believer.

One powerful example of this comes from a man named David—not the biblical king, but a modern-day soldier. After returning from deployment, David carried a crushing sense of guilt over decisions he had made in combat. He avoided church because he believed God couldn't forgive him for what he'd done. One Sunday, his wife convinced him to attend a small gathering where the pastor was teaching from Psalm 51—David's ancient prayer of repentance after his own moral failure. The words *"Wash me, and I will be whiter than snow"* struck him with unexpected force. The story of King David's sin, confession, and forgiveness felt eerily familiar. In that moment, he realized the same God who forgave an adulterous, murderous king could also forgive a soldier burdened by the weight of war. It didn't erase the memories, but it broke the chains of condemnation.

Guilt doesn't always come from dramatic sins. Sometimes it grows from a thousand small failures—a neglected child, a broken friendship, or years of selfishness in a marriage. Maria, a grandmother in her seventies, lived with regret over her strained relationship with her daughter. For decades she justified her actions, but deep down, she knew she had been harsh and unkind. One day while reading the Gospel of Luke, she reached the story of the Prodigal Son. She had read it dozens of times, but this time she saw herself not as the son, but as the father—someone who could choose to extend grace. If God had forgiven her, how could she withhold forgiveness from her own child? She called her daughter that afternoon, apologizing through tears. That phone call began a slow, beautiful reconciliation.

The Bible's way of dealing with guilt is radically different from the worlds. Self-help philosophies often say, "Let go of your guilt," as if it's a matter of personal willpower. But Scripture tells a deeper story: guilt can only be truly lifted when it is placed at the cross. This is why grace is so transformative—it doesn't ignore sin; it cancels its debt.

Grace also turns former failures into testimonies. Paul, once a persecutor of Christians, became one of the most influential apostles in history. He never hid his past; in fact, he often reminded others of it, but always in the context of God's mercy. In 1 Timothy 1:15, he wrote, *"Christ Jesus came into the world to save sinners—of whom I am the worst."* That humility and gratitude fueled his tireless mission.

When a person moves from guilt to grace, they don't just find relief—they find a new identity. They are no longer defined by their worst moments but by God's declaration over them: forgiven, loved, restored. And that truth changes the way they live. People who have truly experienced grace tend to extend it to others, creating a ripple effect of mercy that can heal families, communities, and even entire generations.

The Bible doesn't simply offer instructions for living— it offers the possibility of a completely new start. For the one who feels their past is too dark, God's Word says, *"Though your sins are like scarlet, they shall be as white as snow"* (Isaiah 1:18). From guilt to grace—it is one of the most breathtaking journeys the human soul can take, and the Bible is the faithful map that leads the way.

Chapter 4 – A Light in the Darkness

Darkness can come in many forms—grief, depression, betrayal, poverty, illness, fear. Sometimes it creeps in slowly; other times it crashes over a person like a tidal wave. In the darkest moments, when logic fails and hope feels out of reach, the Bible shines with a light that is both steady and personal. Psalm 119:105 declares, *"Your word is a lamp to my feet and a light to my path."* This is not just poetic language—it is the lived experience of countless people who have found themselves in the night seasons of life.

The Bible's light is unique because it does more than offer comfort; it also gives direction. A flashlight in a storm doesn't just make you feel better—it shows you the way forward. In the same way, Scripture doesn't simply soothe the wounded heart; it guides it toward life, healing, and hope.

One vivid example comes from a woman named Hannah in Eastern Europe. She was a young mother whose husband had been arrested for his Christian faith. Left alone with two small children and no income, she felt abandoned and terrified. One cold evening, she opened the worn Bible her husband had left behind. Her eyes fell on Isaiah 41:10: *"Do not fear, for I am with you; do not be dismayed, for I am your God. I will strengthen you and help you."* She later described that moment as if a candle had been lit inside her soul. The circumstances didn't change immediately, but her outlook did. She held on to that verse like a lifeline, reading it every morning until her husband's release. Years later, she still called it "the night the light came on."

Darkness doesn't always take the form of persecution—it can be personal loss. James, a factory worker in the Midwest, lost his teenage son in a tragic car accident. In the days that followed, he barely spoke, drifting in numbness. A neighbor brought him a meal and a Bible, gently suggesting he read the book of Psalms. At first, the words felt distant. But when James reached Psalm 34:18—*"The Lord is close to the brokenhearted and saves those who are crushed in spirit"*—something broke inside him. It wasn't that his pain disappeared; rather, he realized God was present in his suffering. Over time, those words became a source of quiet strength that carried him through the first year of grief.

There are also moments when the Bible's light exposes the way out of moral darkness. Victor, a businessman in South America, was caught in a web of corruption. He stumbled into a church service while traveling for work, and the pastor preached from 1 John 1:5-7 about walking in the light and confessing sins. That night, Victor returned to his hotel room unable to sleep. The image of walking in the light haunted him. He opened a Gideon

Bible from the nightstand and read the passage again. For the first time, he realized he could leave behind the shadows of dishonesty and step into a life of integrity. It took courage and cost him financially, but he later said, "I would rather live in the light with nothing than in the dark with everything."

The light of Scripture is not a temporary flicker—it is a constant flame. Even in the face of overwhelming darkness, its truth doesn't waver. When the early church faced persecution, they clung to Jesus' words: *"In this world you will have trouble. But take heart! I have overcome the world"* (John 16:33). Those same words still strengthen believers in refugee camps, hospital rooms, prison cells, and quiet bedrooms where tears fall unseen.

Darkness will always exist in this fallen world, but it will never have the final word. The Bible assures us of this in John 1:5: *"The light shines in the darkness, and the darkness has not overcome it."* For those who open its pages in their darkest hour, that promise becomes more than ink on paper—it becomes the light that leads them home.

Chapter 5 – Changing the Heart

The human heart can be stubborn, proud, and resistant to change. When wronged, it clings to bitterness. When corrected, it bristles with defensiveness. When confronted with truth, it can harden like stone. Yet, the Bible has a unique way of penetrating even the most guarded soul. Its words don't simply argue with the mind—they reach the deepest places of the heart; places logic alone cannot touch.

Ezekiel 36:26 records God's promise: *"I will give you a new heart and put a new spirit in you; I will remove from you your heart of stone and give you a heart of flesh."* This transformation is not about polishing up good behavior or adopting religious habits—it is a supernatural change in the very core of a person's desires, attitudes, and priorities.

One powerful example is the story of Mitsuo Fuchida, the Japanese pilot who led the attack on Pearl Harbor in 1941. After the war, Fuchida was disillusioned, bitter, and consumed by hatred toward Americans. His heart was set in stone. But one day, he was handed a pamphlet about a former American POW named Jacob DeShazer. DeShazer had been imprisoned and tortured by the Japanese, yet after reading the Bible in captivity, he had forgiven his captors and returned to Japan as a missionary. Fuchida was stunned—what could cause such a radical change in a man's heart? He bought a Bible to find out. As he read, he encountered the forgiveness of Christ and realized his own need for grace. The man who once led an attack that killed thousands became a follower of Jesus, devoting the rest of his life to sharing the message of peace and reconciliation.

Sometimes the change happens quietly, over time. Maria, a woman from rural Mexico, had been cold and distant toward her neighbors for years, convinced they had wronged her family in business. A local pastor began a Bible study in her village, and though she came reluctantly at first, she found herself drawn to the teachings of Jesus. The turning point came when she read Matthew 5:44—*"Love your enemies and pray for those who persecute you."* At first, the words stung. But as weeks passed, she started praying for the very people she resented. The anger she had carried for decades began to fade, replaced by compassion. Months later, she shocked everyone by inviting those neighbors to her home for a meal. When asked why, she simply said, "The Bible changed my heart."

The Bible can also melt the hardest heart through the power of conviction. In Acts 2, when Peter preached to the crowd about Jesus, the Scripture says they were "cut to the heart" (Acts 2:37). That same piercing conviction still happens today. Daniel, a young man involved in gang violence in Chicago, attended a church service only because a friend promised him lunch afterward. The pastor preached from the story of the Prodigal Son, and when he described the father running to embrace the son who had squandered everything, Daniel felt something break inside. He later said, "It was like the story was about me—and God was the father." That day, he laid down his weapons and began a new life, eventually working with at-risk youth to keep them out of the same cycle he had escaped.

A heart changed by the Bible is more than just softer—it is redirected. Selfishness gives way to generosity, revenge to forgiveness, pride to humility. And while the process can be slow, the results are undeniable. History is filled with men and women whose lives testify that no one is beyond the reach of God's Word. As Hebrews 4:12 reminds us, it is *"sharper than any two-edged sword"*—cutting through excuses, defenses, and facades to reach the true self beneath.

In a world that often says people can't really change, the Bible stands as living proof that they can. Not by sheer willpower or self-improvement plans, but by the renewing power of God's truth. Hearts of stone become hearts of flesh—and those changed hearts often become the greatest agents of change in the lives of others.

Chapter 6 – Overcoming Fear and Anxiety

Fear is one of humanity's oldest and most persistent struggles. It can be rational—protecting us from danger—or irrational, gripping us without warning and stealing our peace. Anxiety often grows from fear, whispering "what if?" until the mind feels trapped in a loop of dread. While life offers countless reasons to be afraid—uncertain finances, health scares, global crises—the Bible repeatedly speaks a stronger message: *Do not fear, for I am with you.*

God's Word addresses fear not by denying the reality of danger, but by placing it in the context of His sovereignty. In Psalm 46, the psalmist declares, *"God is our refuge and strength, an ever-present help in trouble. Therefore, we will not fear, though the earth give way."* The Bible's answer to fear is not blind optimism—it is trust in a God who holds every circumstance in His hands.

One remarkable example comes from Corrie Ten Boom, a Dutch woman who, along with her family, hid Jews during World War II. Arrested and sent to a concentration camp, she endured horrors that would break most people. In her memoir, she describes reading from a smuggled Bible to fellow prisoners, clinging to verses like Psalm 91: *"He who dwells in the shelter of the Most High will rest in the shadow of the Almighty."* Even in the midst of barbed wire, disease, and death, those words became her hiding place. After the war, she traveled the world telling others, "There is no pit so deep that God's love is not deeper still."

Fear and anxiety are not always tied to physical danger—they can also come from the uncertainty of life. Take Sarah, a young mother in the United States who was suddenly laid off from her job. Her mind spiraled with panic: How would she pay rent? How would she feed her children? One night, she couldn't sleep and opened her Bible to Matthew 6. As she read Jesus' words—*"Do not worry about your life... Look at the birds of the air; they do not sow or reap... and yet your heavenly Father feeds them"*—her breathing slowed. She realized her anxiety came from trying to control what was beyond her power. That night, she prayed for the first time in months, releasing her fears to God. Within a week, she received a part-time job offer that became the stepping stone to full employment.

Even seasoned believers can find themselves battling anxiety. Mark, a missionary in Asia, faced constant government scrutiny. Each knock on the door could have been the one that sent him to prison. His lifeline was memorized Scripture. Each morning, before stepping outside, he recited Isaiah 26:3: *"You will keep in perfect peace those whose minds are steadfast, because they trust in you."* He later said, "I didn't feel brave most days—but the Word reminded me God was bigger than the fear."

The Bible's approach to fear is not a one-time fix but an ongoing practice. By regularly meditating on God's promises, fear loses its grip. As 2 Timothy 1:7 says, *"God has not given us a spirit of fear, but of power and of love and of a sound mind."* The more a believer's mind is filled with truth, the less room there is for anxiety to dominate.

In every generation, the people of God have faced threats, uncertainty, and hardship. Yet, those who have rooted their hearts in Scripture have found a peace the world cannot give. Fear may still knock at the door, but when the light of God's Word fills the room, it cannot stay.

Fear and anxiety are among the most common struggles people face, touching every age, culture, and background. They can paralyze decisions, steal joy, and isolate us from others. The Bible, however, offers a powerful antidote—not by promising a life free from fear, but by showing how to face fear with faith and find peace amid uncertainty.

Understanding Fear and Anxiety

Fear is a natural response to danger, meant to protect us. Anxiety, however, is often a persistent, excessive worry about the future or things beyond our control. Both can become destructive when they dominate our minds and hearts.

The Bible acknowledges the reality of fear but consistently encourages believers to trust God instead of succumbing to worry. One of the most repeated commands is, *"Do not be afraid."* It appears over 365 times, a daily reminder that God's presence replaces fear.

God's Presence as Our Refuge

Psalm 46:1 declares, *"God is our refuge and strength, an ever-present help in trouble."* This verse reminds us that fear loses its power when we recognize God as our protector and helper. In moments of anxiety, turning to God through prayer and scripture can bring immediate comfort.

A woman named Lisa struggled with panic attacks for years. She found relief when she memorized verses like Isaiah 41:10: *"So do not fear, for I am with you; do not be dismayed, for I am your God."* Repeating these promises helped her shift her focus from fear to faith.

Casting Our Cares on God

1 Peter 5:7 urges believers to *"cast all your anxiety on him because he cares for you."* This is not a passive

surrender but an active decision to hand over worries to God. When we do this, we invite His peace to guard our hearts.

Prayer plays a crucial role. Philippians 4:6–7 teaches, *"Do not be anxious about anything, but in every situation, by prayer and petition, with thanksgiving, present your requests to God. And the peace of God, which transcends all understanding, will guard your hearts and your minds in Christ Jesus."*

The Example of Jesus

Jesus Himself experienced deep distress and anxiety. In the Garden of Gethsemane, He prayed, *"My soul is overwhelmed with sorrow to the point of death"* (Matthew 26:38). Yet He chose to submit His fears to the Father's will. This example shows that fear is not sin, but surrendering fear to God is faith.

Replacing Fear with Faith

Faith is the key to overcoming fear. Hebrews 11:1 defines faith as *"confidence in what we hope for and assurance about what we do not see."* When we trust God's promises, fear begins to lose its grip.

Joshua 1:9 commands, *"Be strong and courageous. Do not be afraid; do not be discouraged, for the Lord your God will be with you wherever you go."* Courage is not the absence of fear, but acting in faith despite fear.

Practical Steps to Combat Anxiety

- **Meditate on Scripture:** Filling the mind with God's promises replaces worry with truth.
- **Prayer and Thanksgiving:** Regularly talking with God and thanking Him shifts focus from problems to provision.
- **Community Support:** Sharing fears with trusted believers brings encouragement and prayer.
- **Mindfulness and Rest:** God designed rest for body and mind. Taking time to slow down can reduce anxiety.

A Real-Life Testimony: James' Journey Through Anxiety

James was overwhelmed by anxiety after losing his job unexpectedly. Sleepless nights and constant worry consumed him. One evening, a friend shared Psalm 94:19: *"When anxiety was great within me, your consolation brought me joy."*

James began attending a church support group and reading the Bible daily. He practiced prayer, breathing exercises, and found comfort in fellowship. Slowly, his anxiety lessened. James is now the mentor for others struggling with fear, sharing how God's peace transformed his life.

Closing Reflection

Fear and anxiety are part of the human experience, but they do not have to define us. The Bible calls us to replace fear with faith, worry with worship, and panic with prayer. When we choose to trust God—acknowledging His power, presence, and promises—we unlock a peace that stands firm amid life's storms. As Isaiah 41:13 assures us, *"For I am the Lord your God who takes hold of your right hand and says to you, do not fear; I will help you."*

Chapter 7 – Breaking Chains

Chains don't always rattle loudly. Some are visible—addictions, destructive habits, and blatant sin. Others are quieter but just as strong—patterns of selfishness, greed, lust, or anger that hold people captive. These chains can last for years, convincing a person they will never change. Yet, time and again, the Bible has proven to be a key that unlocks those shackles, offering not just temporary relief but lasting freedom.

Jesus Himself declared this purpose in Luke 4:18: *"He has sent me to proclaim freedom for the prisoners and recovery of sight for the blind, to set the oppressed free."* The chains may be physical, emotional, or spiritual, but the message is the same—no bondage is too strong for God's Word to break.

One striking story is that of Augustine, a young man in the 4th century whose life was consumed by immorality and reckless living. Despite his mother's prayers, he seemed set on a path of self-destruction. One day, in deep inner turmoil, he heard a child's voice singing, *"Take and read, take and read."* He picked up a Bible and opened it at random to Romans 13:13-14: *"Let us behave decently... not in carousing and drunkenness, not in sexual immorality and debauchery... Rather, clothe yourselves with the Lord Jesus Christ."* Those words cut him to the core. That day, he surrendered his life to Christ, and his transformation was so complete that he became one of the most influential Christian thinkers in history.

In more recent times, the story of Brian, a man in Canada, shows the Bible's power to break addiction. Brian had been addicted to meth for over a decade, cycling through jail, rehab, and the streets. In prison, he was given a small New Testament by a chaplain. At first, he used its thin pages to roll cigarettes. But one day, before tearing out another page, he decided to read it. The verse was John 8:36: *"So if the Son sets you free, you will be free indeed."* For the first time in years, he dared to believe freedom was possible. Slowly, as he read the Gospels daily, the cravings lost their hold. When he was released, he joined a church, got clean, and began working with others trapped in addiction. He often says, "The Word didn't just get me out of prison—it got prison out of me."

Not all chains are chemical. Emily, a young woman in Australia, was trapped in a cycle of bitterness toward her estranged father. Every attempt to forgive him felt hollow. One evening, she read Ephesians 4:31-32: *"Get rid of all bitterness, rage and anger... Be kind and compassionate to one another, forgiving each other, just as in Christ God forgave you."* The words "just as" hit her hardest—if God could forgive her fully, how could she withhold forgiveness from another? It wasn't easy, and it didn't happen overnight, but she began praying for her father. Months later, she wrote him a letter that began the process of reconciliation. In her words, "The Bible didn't just tell me to forgive—it gave me the power to do it."

When the Bible speaks of freedom, it's not a vague spiritual concept—it is practical, tangible, and life-changing. It addresses the root, not just the symptom. Addiction programs may help manage behavior, but Scripture transforms the heart, replacing destructive desires with holy ones.

The chains we carry may be heavy, but they are not permanent. Acts 16 tells of Paul and Silas in prison, singing hymns when an earthquake flung the doors wide open. In a spiritual sense, the Bible often works the same way—shaking the very foundations of our prisons until the locks break and the captives walk free. For anyone still bound, the message is clear: the chains can be broken, and the Bible shows the way out.

Chains are powerful symbols. They represent captivity, restriction, and bondage—whether physical, emotional, or spiritual. Throughout the Bible, breaking chains stands for freedom: freedom from sin, fear, addiction, and oppression. The Bible not only acknowledges the chains that bind us but also provides the key to breaking them and living in freedom.

The Reality of Chains

Many people today experience chains in various forms—addictions, harmful habits, guilt, fear, toxic relationships, and past traumas. These chains may feel invisible, but their weight can be just as heavy as literal imprisonment. They limit potential, steal joy, and hold people back from the abundant life God desires for them.

The apostle Paul described sin as a form of slavery, writing, *"For sin shall no longer be your master, because you are not under the law, but under grace"* (Romans 6:14). This spiritual bondage can seem impossible to escape through human effort alone.

Jesus Came to Set Us Free

Jesus' mission was described in Luke 4:18–19, where He quoted Isaiah: *"He has sent me to proclaim freedom for the prisoners and recovery of sight for the blind, to set the oppressed free."* This is not just poetic language—it is a declaration that through Jesus, chains can be broken.

When Jesus encountered individuals bound by sickness, demonic oppression, or sin, He demonstrated His authority by breaking their chains instantly. His power to free goes beyond the physical to address deep spiritual and emotional bondage.

The Role of Repentance and Forgiveness

Breaking chains often begins with repentance—a turning away from what binds us and turning toward God. This act opens the door for forgiveness, which is crucial in breaking the chains of guilt and shame.

Consider Peter, who denied Jesus three times but was restored and freed from his guilt through Jesus' forgiveness (John 21:15–17). His story encourages believers that no chain is too strong for God's grace.

Overcoming Addictions and Strongholds

Addictions—whether to substances, behaviors, or destructive thought patterns—are chains that many struggle with. The Bible offers hope for those trapped in such cycles. 2 Corinthians 10:4–5 reminds us that the weapons God provides *"have divine power to demolish strongholds."*

Breaking chains requires practical steps alongside spiritual surrender: seeking accountability, professional help when needed, and relying on God's strength daily. No one is expected to break chains alone.

Freedom Through the Holy Spirit

The Holy Spirit empowers believers to live free lives. Galatians 5:1 declares, *"It is for freedom that Christ has set us free. Stand firm, then, and do not let yourselves be burdened again by a yoke of slavery."*

This freedom is not just a one-time event but a daily choice to walk in the Spirit and resist returning to old patterns. The Spirit guides, convicts, and strengthens us in the fight for freedom.

The Power of Community

Chains are often broken best in the company of others. Biblical community provides encouragement, support, and accountability. The early church met regularly to encourage one another in faith and freedom (Acts 2:42–47).

Stories abound of people finding liberation through trusted relationships—small groups, mentors, or pastors who walk alongside them on the journey to freedom.

A Real-Life Testimony: Jessica's Freedom

Jessica battled a 15-year addiction to prescription drugs. She felt trapped, ashamed, and hopeless. After hitting rock bottom, she turned to God in desperation. Through a church recovery ministry, she found healing.

Jessica recalls, "The chains felt unbreakable. But as I surrendered my pain, my fear, and my addiction to Jesus, I began to feel a peace and strength I had never known. The Holy Spirit gave me the courage to face each day. The support of my church family helped me stay strong. Today, I'm free—no longer a prisoner to my past."

Closing Reflection

Chains, no matter how strong, are never beyond God's power to break. Through Jesus, we are offered freedom—freedom from sin, shame, addiction, and fear. This freedom requires faith, surrender, and often the support of community, but it is always possible. As Paul wrote in Galatians 5:13, *"You, my brothers and sisters, were called to be free. But do not use your freedom to indulge the flesh; rather, serve one another humbly in love."* True freedom is not only breaking chains but living in love and service.

Chapter 8 – A New Purpose

One of the most disorienting feelings in life is to drift without direction. Many people live years—sometimes decades—without a clear sense of "why" they are here. Careers may provide income, hobbies may bring momentary enjoyment, but deep purpose is something more: it's the conviction that your life is part of a larger story. The Bible has a remarkable way of awakening that conviction, showing people that they were not made by accident, but for a divine purpose that matters in eternity.

The pages of Scripture are filled with people who were going about their ordinary—or even misguided—lives when God interrupted them with a new mission. Moses was tending sheep when God called him from a burning bush to lead an entire nation to freedom (Exodus 3). Peter and Andrew were casting nets when Jesus invited them to become "fishers of men" (Matthew 4:19). Saul was on his way to arrest Christians when the risen Christ met him on the road to Damascus, transforming him into Paul, one of history's greatest missionaries (Acts 9).

Each of these men had a path they thought was their future—until the Word of God redirected it entirely.

A modern example comes from a woman named Lillian, a retired nurse in the United Kingdom. After her husband passed away, she felt useless and forgotten. Her days were filled with television, naps, and an occasional lunch with friends, but her heart felt hollow. One afternoon, she picked up her dusty Bible and began reading the book of James. She paused at James 1:27: *"Religion that God our Father accepts as pure and faultless is this: to look after orphans and widows in their distress."* She realized that even as a widow herself, she could be part of God's care for others. She began volunteering at a community center, offering medical advice to low-income families. What started as a few hours a week became a thriving outreach ministry. Lillian often says, "I thought my story was over—but the Bible gave me a new chapter."

For some, purpose comes in the form of radical redirection. Carlos, a young man in Brazil, dreamed only of making money. He left his rural home for the city, working long hours and climbing the corporate ladder. Yet with every promotion, the emptiness grew. Late one night, unable to sleep, he opened the Bible his mother had given him and read Philippians 3:7-8, where Paul writes, *"Whatever were gains to me I now consider loss for the sake of Christ."* Those words unsettled him. Over the following weeks, he wrestled with the idea that his life's pursuit might be meaningless apart from God. Eventually, he left his job to start a nonprofit that provides job training and shares the Gospel with at-risk youth. "For the first time," he says, "I'm building something that will outlast me."

The Bible also has a way of awakening purpose in small but equally profound ways. Not every calling means changing careers or moving to another country. Purpose might mean being the first in your family to walk with integrity, raising children to love God, or faithfully serving behind the scenes in ways the world will never applaud. The story of Anna in Luke 2 is a reminder of this truth. She was a prophetess who spent her days in the temple, worshiping, fasting, and praying. She never traveled the world or led armies, but her faithful life prepared her to witness the arrival of the Messiah. Purpose is not measured by applause but by obedience.

Even those who feel they've wasted years can find new direction in the Bible. Thomas, a former gang member in California, spent most of his twenties in and out of prison. At 33, he began reading the book of Jonah and was struck by the fact that God gave Jonah a second chance to obey, even after he ran away. Thomas realized it wasn't too late for him either. He began mentoring younger men still in the gang life, guiding them toward Christ. Today, he leads a Bible study in the same neighborhood where he once caused harm. "My purpose now," he says, "is to help others avoid the mistakes I made—and to tell them God can use anyone."

Psalm 138:8 says, *"The Lord will fulfill his purpose for me."* This promise is not limited by age, past mistakes, or present circumstances. The Bible teaches that every believer has a role in God's grand story, and discovering that role fills life with meaning far greater than personal comfort or success.

Purpose gives suffering a new frame. It turns hardships into training grounds, setbacks into stepping stones, and even failures into testimonies. When someone encounters the God of Scripture, they discover that their days are not random and their work is not in vain. Their life becomes part of something that began before they were born and will continue long after they are gone.

The truth is, the Bible doesn't just give people a new purpose—it gives them the right purpose. And once that purpose takes root, it reshapes everything: how they spend their time, how they view their resources, and how they measure success. For those who once drifted without direction, the moment the Word of God reveals their calling is like the turning of a compass needle toward true north. They finally know where they are headed—and why.

Chapter 9 – Building Moral Foundations

Morality shapes the way individuals relate to themselves, to others, and to society at large. It forms the invisible framework for decisions, behaviors, and the very culture in which people live. For many, this framework begins in childhood, shaped by family, education, and community values. Yet for billions worldwide, the Bible serves as the bedrock of moral teaching—a timeless source of principles that build character and guide ethical choices across generations.

At the heart of biblical morality is the call to love—love for God and love for neighbor. When Jesus summarized the Law and the Prophets in Matthew 22:37-39, he said, *"Love the Lord your God with all your heart... and love your neighbor as yourself."* This simple yet profound principle forms the foundation for countless ethical teachings throughout Scripture. It calls people away from selfishness, dishonesty, and cruelty toward lives marked by integrity, compassion, and justice.

Consider the story of John Newton, once a slave trader whose life was marked by exploitation and greed. After encountering the Bible's message of grace, his heart changed, and he became a fervent abolitionist. His transformation shows how biblical morality can overturn not just personal habits but systemic injustice. Newton's moral foundation, rooted in Scripture, led him to challenge the accepted norms of his time and advocate for the dignity and freedom of all people.

The Bible also addresses everyday moral decisions. Proverbs, often called the book of wisdom, offers practical advice on honesty, humility, diligence, and kindness. For example, Proverbs 12:22 declares, *"The Lord detests lying lips, but he delights in people who are trustworthy."* In communities where the Bible's moral teachings take root, studies often show lower crime rates and higher levels of social trust. Moral foundations shaped by Scripture create cultures where promises are kept, businesses act ethically, and neighbors care for one another.

In a modern context, consider the story of Grace, a small-business owner in Kenya. She grew up in a community where corruption was common, and cutting corners was seen as necessary to survive. After attending a church Bible study focused on the Ten Commandments, Grace was convicted to run her business with honesty and fairness—even when it meant slower profits. Over time, her reputation for integrity attracted loyal customers and even inspired other business owners to follow her example. Grace says, "The Bible gave me the courage to stand firm when it was easier to take the easy way."

The Bible's moral foundation also shapes leadership and governance. The early American founders, many influenced by biblical principles, wrote laws and documents reflecting the belief in human dignity, justice, and equality before the law. The idea that all people are created in God's image (Genesis 1:27) has been foundational in movements for human rights worldwide.

However, building a moral foundation on the Bible is not about rigid rule-following or judgmental attitudes. Rather, it is about cultivating hearts aligned with God's character—hearts that value mercy (Micah 6:8), seek justice (Isaiah 1:17), and practice humility (Philippians 2:3). When this internal transformation happens, moral choices flow naturally from a desire to honor God and serve others.

The Bible also acknowledges that no one is perfect, and moral growth is a lifelong journey. Paul's letters remind believers to continually put off selfishness and put on Christ-like virtues (Ephesians 4:22-24). This ongoing process creates communities where grace and truth coexist, helping individuals persevere in their moral walk.

In a world often marked by moral confusion and shifting values, the Bible provides a steady compass. Its timeless principles have shaped lives, families, and nations by providing a foundation on which to build trustworthy, just, and compassionate character. For those who build their moral lives on the Bible, the result is not just personal goodness but a ripple effect that influences society for the better.

Chapter 10 – The Power of Forgiveness

Forgiveness is one of the most powerful and transformative themes woven throughout the Bible. It is both a divine command and a profound gift that changes lives at the deepest levels. To forgive is to release someone from the debt of offense, bitterness, and anger—an act that frees not only the person forgiven but also the one who forgives. Without forgiveness, relationships remain fractured, wounds fester, and people carry burdens that weigh heavily on their souls.

The Bible's teaching on forgiveness begins with God Himself. In Ephesians 4:32, believers are urged to *"Be kind and compassionate to one another, forgiving each other, just as in Christ God forgave you."* This is not presented as an optional virtue, but as a foundational way of life, modeled perfectly by Jesus Christ on the cross. His sacrifice provided the ultimate example of forgiving others—even those who caused Him unimaginable pain.

Consider the story of Immaculée Ilibagiza, a survivor of the Rwandan genocide. During the brutal massacre, she lost most of her family and lived in hiding for months. After surviving, she faced the unimaginable task of forgiving the men who had killed her loved ones. Drawing strength from her Christian faith and the Bible, particularly passages about God's forgiveness, Immaculée chose to forgive. Her decision did not erase the horrors but released her from the poison of hatred. Today, she travels the world sharing her story and advocating reconciliation, showing how forgiveness can bring healing even from the darkest places.

Forgiveness also plays a critical role in healing personal relationships. In the United States, Mark and Susan had been married for fifteen years when an affair shattered their trust. Both were devastated, and divorce seemed inevitable. However, through counseling rooted in biblical principles, they began to understand forgiveness as a choice and a process, not just a feeling. Verses like Colossians 3:13—*"Bear with each other and forgive one another if any of you has a grievance against someone. Forgive as the Lord forgave you."*—became their anchor. Over time, forgiveness softened hearts, restored communication, and rebuilt their marriage. Their journey illustrates that forgiveness is often the first step toward restoration.

The Bible also challenges believers to forgive even when it feels impossible. Jesus taught Peter to forgive *"seventy times seven"* times (Matthew 18:22), emphasizing that forgiveness is not limited or conditional. This radical call to forgiveness defies natural human instincts for revenge or resentment, but it offers freedom from the corrosive effects of holding onto offense.

Forgiveness transforms communities as well. In post-apartheid South Africa, the Truth and Reconciliation Commission embodied biblical forgiveness on a national scale. Victims and perpetrators faced each other in a process that sought truth, justice, and the possibility of forgiveness. Many participants cited Christian faith and Scripture as sources of courage to forgive and seek healing. This example demonstrates how biblical forgiveness can transcend individual hearts and foster societal renewal.

Yet, forgiveness does not mean forgetting or excusing wrongdoing. The Bible recognizes justice and the consequences of sin. But it insists that mercy and grace must accompany justice to break cycles of hatred and violence. Forgiveness releases the victim from bondage and opens the door for healing and reconciliation, though it often requires time, prayer, and humility.

The power of forgiveness in the Bible is transformative because it reflects the heart of God. As believers forgive others, they mirror God's mercy and open their own hearts to His healing grace. Forgiveness breaks chains, restores relationships, and ushers in peace that surpasses understanding. It is a central way the Bible changes lives—not only by healing the wounds of the past but by creating a future marked by hope and reconciliation.

Few human experiences are as freeing—or as challenging—as forgiveness. The Bible presents forgiveness not as an optional virtue, but as a core command and a reflection of God's own character. From Genesis to Revelation, it is a recurring theme: God forgives, and those who have been forgiven are called to extend that same grace to others.

Jesus made forgiveness central to His teaching. In the Lord's Prayer, He instructed His followers to pray, *"Forgive us our debts, as we also have forgiven our debtors"* (Matthew 6:12). This simple yet profound request ties God's forgiveness of us directly to our willingness to forgive others. To modern ears, this may seem like a moral ideal—but in biblical terms, it's a spiritual necessity. Unforgiveness is not just a relational barrier; it's a spiritual one.

The Weight We Carry Without Forgiveness

Unforgiveness is like carrying a heavy backpack filled with stones. Every hurt, every betrayal, every insult adds another weight. Over time, this burden saps energy, clouds judgment, and hardens hearts. Some try to justify their bitterness, believing it protects them from further harm. In reality, it locks them into the past, allowing the offense to define their future. The Bible's call to forgive is not about excusing wrongdoing, but about releasing the poison before it destroys us.

One man named Michael carried deep resentment for years after a close business partner stole from him and left him bankrupt. Even after rebuilding his life, he found himself reliving the betrayal, unable to trust anyone fully. Reading Jesus' parable of the unforgiving servant in Matthew 18 struck him deeply: he realized that his own sins against God were far greater than any wrong committed against him, yet God had released him from the debt completely. That truth broke the chains of resentment, and though reconciliation with his former partner was not possible, Michael forgave him in his heart—and found peace for the first time in decades.

The Example of Jesus

The greatest demonstration of forgiveness in the Bible occurred at the cross. As Jesus hung between two criminals, mocked and tortured, He prayed, *"Father, forgive them, for they do not know what they are doing"* (Luke 23:34). This was not passive acceptance of evil, but an active choice to release the debt of those who had wronged Him—before they had apologized, and while they were still in the act of committing the offense.

This example challenges believers to forgive even when the offender does not acknowledge the harm. Forgiveness, in this sense, is more about the condition of the forgiver's heart than the offender's response. It is a spiritual act of entrusting justice to God rather than seeking personal revenge.

Forgiveness in Relationships

Forgiveness transforms marriages, friendships, and families. Many relationships break not from a single offense but from an accumulation of unresolved hurts. The Bible's approach—*"Bear with each other and forgive one another... Forgive as the Lord forgave you"* (Colossians 3:13)—reminds us that grace must be ongoing.

Consider the story of Sarah and Emily, two sisters who hadn't spoken for over ten years after a bitter dispute over their parents' inheritance. Both felt justified in their anger. Then Sarah, after attending a Bible study on reconciliation, wrote a letter admitting her part in the conflict and expressing a desire to heal the relationship. Emily wept as she read it. The process of rebuilding trust took time, but today they speak weekly and often pray together—something neither thought possible.

Forgiveness as a Testimony

In a world that often values retaliation, forgiveness is a striking witness to the power of the gospel. Stories abound of believers who have forgiven in unimaginable circumstances: a parent extending grace to a drunk driver who killed their child, or a community choosing reconciliation after a violent attack. Such acts defy human logic and point unmistakably to a higher power at work.

One powerful modern example comes from Rwanda, where survivors of the 1994 genocide have publicly embraced those who murdered their family members. Many testify that their ability to do so flows directly from understanding Christ's forgiveness for them. In their words, "We forgive because we were forgiven first."

Forgiveness Does Not Mean Forgetting

It's important to note that biblical forgiveness does not demand pretending an offense never happened or placing oneself in harm's way again. Forgiveness releases the offender from personal vengeance, but boundaries and wisdom may still be necessary. Even God's forgiveness does not always remove earthly consequences, but it does restore relationship and open the door to healing.

The Freedom Forgiveness Brings

Ultimately, forgiveness is an act of faith. It trusts that God's justice is perfect, that His grace is sufficient, and that His love can heal even the deepest wounds. It frees the heart from bitterness and opens the door for reconciliation where possible. Most of all, it reflects the very heart of the gospel: a God who loves us enough to cancel our unpayable debt and invite us into a restored relationship with Him.

Forgiveness is not easy—it is often a process, not a one-time event. But each act of letting go moves us closer to the life God intends for us: a life marked by peace, joy, and the ability to love without chains.

A Real-Life Testimony: Anna's Choice

Anna's life changed forever when her teenage son was killed in a robbery gone wrong. The young man who pulled the trigger was caught and sentenced to prison. For years, Anna lived with an unshakable ache, replaying the "what ifs" in her mind. At church one Sunday, she heard the story of Jesus forgiving His executioners. She wrestled with that idea—*How could I ever forgive someone who took my son?*

Months later, Anna made a choice. She visited the prison and asked to meet the young man. When she looked into his eyes, she saw fear, shame, and a brokenness not unlike her own. With tears streaming, she told him, "I forgive you. I will not let this hate destroy me."

That day, a weight lifted. She began writing him letters, sharing Scripture, and praying for him. Over time, he gave his life to Christ. Anna says, "Forgiveness didn't bring my son back, but it brought me back to life."

Chapter 11 – The Strength of Faith

Faith is the lifeblood of the Christian experience, a powerful force that sustains, empowers, and transforms individuals facing life's most daunting challenges. The Bible presents faith not simply as belief in God's existence, but as confident trust in His character and promises, especially when circumstances are uncertain or painful. Hebrews 11, often called the "Faith Hall of Fame," chronicles stories of ordinary people who relied on faith to overcome fear, trials, and doubt, setting a timeless example for all believers.

Take the story of Daniel, who lived in exile in Babylon yet refused to compromise his faith. When ordered to worship idols, he stood firm despite the threat of the lions' den. His unwavering trust in God's protection did not always mean a painless path, but his faith provided strength that transcended fear and gave him courage to act rightly. This biblical example has inspired millions to hold fast to faith amid persecution and uncertainty.

In modern times, consider the story of Heather, a young woman diagnosed with a life-threatening illness. Faced with surgery and long treatment, she described how her faith anchored her through moments of overwhelming fear. Scriptures such as Isaiah 41:10—*"Do not fear, for I am with you; do not be dismayed, for I am your God."*—became her refuge. Heather says that faith didn't instantly remove her pain, but it gave her a deep peace and the strength to endure. For her, faith was like an unshakable foundation beneath the storm.

Faith also fuels hope and perseverance. The Apostle Paul, imprisoned and beaten for preaching the Gospel, wrote in Romans 8:38-39 about the inseparable love of God. His faith gave him the resilience to face suffering with joy, knowing that ultimate victory was assured. This perspective has encouraged countless believers facing personal hardships—from poverty and discrimination to addiction and loss—to keep moving forward.

Faith can also bring about miraculous change. Mary Johnson's son was murdered in a violent attack, leaving her devastated and broken. Yet, through her Bible study, she encountered Romans 12:21: *"Do not be overcome by evil, but overcome evil with good."* Choosing faith over bitterness, she founded a ministry that promotes forgiveness and reconciliation in communities plagued by violence. Her story demonstrates how faith can convert pain into purpose and restore broken lives.

But faith is not merely about grand acts or miracles—it shapes daily living. It influences decisions, relationships, and how believers interpret life's events. Faith invites trust in God's sovereignty and goodness, even when the future is unknown. As Proverbs 3:5-6 advises, *"Trust in the Lord with all your heart and lean not on your own understanding; in all your ways submit to him, and he will make your paths straight."*

Importantly, faith is often a journey, marked by doubts and questions as well as conviction. The Bible records moments when even heroes of faith wrestled with uncertainty. Yet, their willingness to keep seeking and trusting despite doubts provides a relatable and encouraging example for believers today.

In a world where certainty is rare and fear common, the strength of faith stands as a beacon of hope. It is a supernatural resource, empowering believers to face trials, overcome obstacles, and live lives marked by courage, peace, and purpose. The Bible's message about faith is not just theoretical—it is practical and transformative, changing lives by inviting people into a trusting relationship with God that sustains them through every season.

Chapter 12 – Finding Peace in Troubled Times

Peace is a longing deeply embedded in the human heart. Yet, peace is often elusive, especially when life brings chaos, loss, and uncertainty. The Bible offers a peace that transcends circumstances—a profound inner calm that does not depend on the absence of trouble but on the presence of God. This peace has changed countless lives, providing comfort and strength when the world feels anything but peaceful.

Jesus spoke of this peace in John 14:27: *"Peace I leave with you; my peace I give you. I do not give to you as the world gives. Do not let your hearts be troubled and do not be afraid."* Unlike the fleeting calm offered by worldly solutions, the peace Jesus promises is enduring and supernatural.

Consider the story of Naomi, a woman who lost her husband and two sons in quick succession. Bereft and alone, she felt overwhelmed by grief. Yet, in her darkest moments, she clung to Psalm 34:18: *"The Lord is close to the brokenhearted and saves those who are crushed in spirit."* Through prayer and Scripture, Naomi found a peace that did not erase her sorrow but gave her strength to face each day. Her story reminds us that biblical peace often coexists with pain—it transforms how pain is endured.

In more recent times, Ahmed, a refugee fleeing war-torn Syria, faced unimaginable hardships. Displaced, separated from family, and uncertain about the future, he was introduced to the Bible by aid workers. Isaiah 26:3—*"You will keep in perfect peace those whose minds are steadfast, because they trust in you"*—became a source of daily comfort. Ahmed says that trusting God's promises helped him find peace amid the chaos, giving him hope and resilience.

Peace also plays a crucial role in mental health. Anxiety and worry plague millions, often exacerbated by feelings of helplessness. The Apostle Paul's words in Philippians 4:6-7 provide a powerful antidote: *"Do not be anxious about anything, but in every situation, by prayer and petition, with thanksgiving, present your requests to God. And the peace of God, which transcends all understanding, will guard your hearts and your minds in Christ Jesus."* Believers who practice this discipline often testify to an inner peace that sustains them through stress and trials.

Moreover, peace is not only an individual experience but a gift for communities. Biblical teachings encourage reconciliation, forgiveness, and justice—all essential for peace among people. The work of peacemakers, inspired by Scripture, has changed nations torn by conflict, demonstrating the Bible's power to restore broken relationships and societies.

Yet, finding peace does not mean escaping difficulties. The Bible acknowledges that life will have troubles (John 16:33). But it invites believers to anchor themselves in God's presence, *finding peace that the world cannot take away. This peace steady's* hearts, heals wounds, and empowers people to live with courage and hope, even in the storm.

For those seeking peace today, the Bible remains a steadfast guide—a source of comfort and assurance that true peace is possible, no matter the external circumstances. Through its promises, teachings, and stories, it changes lives by replacing fear with calm, confusion with clarity, and despair with hope.

Peace is one of the most sought-after treasures in life. People chase it through financial security, relationships, vacations, or personal achievements, yet often find that peace slips away when life becomes uncertain or painful. The Bible offers a very different kind of peace—one that does not depend on circumstances, but flows from a relationship with God Himself.

Jesus spoke directly to this need when He told His disciples, *"Peace I leave with you; my peace I give you. I do not give to you as the world gives"* (John 14:27). This was not a poetic phrase spoken in calm surroundings; it was a promise given just before His arrest, trial, and crucifixion. He wanted them to understand that true peace could exist even in the middle of chaos.

The Nature of Biblical Peace

In the Bible, peace is more than the absence of conflict. The Hebrew word *shalom* describes wholeness, well-being, and harmony with God, others, and ourselves. It's a settled state of mind that comes from knowing God is in control, even when we are not.

This peace is not fragile; it does not crumble when the news is bad, the bills pile up, or a diagnosis changes the course of life. Instead, it is anchored in the unchanging nature of God. The prophet Isaiah declared, *"You will keep in perfect peace those whose minds are steadfast, because they trust in you"* (Isaiah 26:3).

Peace in the Midst of Uncertainty

One of the hardest times to find peace is when the future is unclear. Financial hardship, broken relationships, and global crises can make it feel like life is spinning out of control. Yet again and again, Scripture calls believers to trust in the Lord's sovereignty.

Consider Mark's account of Jesus calming the storm (Mark 4:35–41). The disciples, seasoned fishermen, were terrified as the wind roared and waves crashed into their boat. Jesus, however, was asleep. When they woke Him, He rebuked the storm and it became completely calm. His question, *"Why are you so afraid? Do you still have no faith?"*, reminds us that peace comes not from controlling the storm but from knowing the One who commands it.

Peace in the Midst of Loss

Grief is one of the deepest trials of life, and yet even here, the Bible offers hope. The apostle Paul wrote of a *"peace of God, which transcends all understanding"* (Philippians 4:7)—a peace that doesn't erase pain, but carries us through it.

A man named Robert experienced this when his wife of 40 years passed away unexpectedly. In the first weeks, he felt like he was walking through darkness. Then one morning, during his daily Bible reading, he came to Psalm 34:18: *"The Lord is close to the brokenhearted and saves those who are crushed in spirit."* In that moment, Robert said it was as though God wrapped His arms around him. The grief remained, but a steady calm took root in his heart—assurance that he was not alone.

Choosing Peace Through Prayer

Peace often requires a deliberate choice to turn anxieties over to God. Philippians 4:6–7 gives a clear pathway: *"Do not be anxious about anything, but in every situation, by prayer and petition, with thanksgiving, present your requests to God. And the peace of God... will guard your hearts and your minds in Christ Jesus."*

This is not simply a call to say a quick prayer and move on—it is an invitation to exchange worry for worship, to release control and rest in God's care. Many believers testify that when they bring every concern, no matter how small, before God, they feel a tangible shift in their spirit.

Peace as a Witness

In troubled times, peace stands out. When the world expects panic, the calm of a believer can become a testimony of faith. Friends, family, and co-workers may ask, "How can you be so at peace?"—opening the door to share about the One who gives it.

During a recent economic downturn, a business owner named Linda faced the possibility of closing her shop. Yet instead of despair, she prayed with her employees, encouraging them to trust God together. Though the business eventually closed, her steady faith inspired two employees to begin reading the Bible, curious about the source of her peace.

The Promise of Lasting Peace

The peace offered in the Bible is not temporary; it is part of God's eternal plan. Revelation describes a future where there will be no more mourning, crying, or pain, for God will dwell with His people in perfect harmony (Revelation 21:3–4). That hope allows believers to walk through present troubles with their eyes on the horizon of eternity.

A Real-Life Testimony: Maria's Storm

Maria lived in a war-torn region where the sound of gunfire was part of daily life. Fear was her constant companion until a neighbor invited her to a small Bible study. There she read Psalm 46:1–2 for the first time: *"God is our refuge and strength, an ever-present help in trouble. Therefore we will not fear, though the earth give way..."*

That verse became her lifeline. Even as bombs fell nearby, she prayed those words and felt a calm she couldn't explain. One night, when others fled in panic, she stayed and comforted a crying child, whispering, "God is with us." Years later, Maria says, "The war did not end quickly, but the war inside my heart did. His peace never left me."

Closing Reflection

Maria's story echoes the promise Jesus gave in John 16:33: *"In this world you will have trouble. But take heart! I have overcome the world."* The storms of life are inevitable—whether they come in the form of war, illness, loss, or uncertainty—but the peace of Christ is unshakable. It is not the absence of trouble, but the presence of God in the midst of it. Those who place their trust in Him find a peace that the world cannot give and cannot take away. And in that peace, they discover the quiet strength to face whatever comes, knowing they are never alone.

Chapter 13 – The Role of Prayer

Prayer is the intimate conversation between a person and God—a lifeline that connects the finite human heart to the infinite Creator. Across the pages of the Bible, prayer emerges as a powerful force that changes lives by fostering relationship, providing guidance, offering comfort, and opening channels for divine intervention. Far beyond a ritual or routine, prayer invites believers into a dynamic partnership with God.

The Bible shows prayer in every season of life: in times of joy, grief, confusion, and triumph. King David's Psalms give us some of the most profound examples of prayer's emotional range—from cries for help (*"Hear my cry, O God"* Psalm 61:1) to songs of praise (*"The Lord is my shepherd"* Psalm 23:1). These prayers reveal how deeply personal and transformative communication with God can be.

One remarkable story is that of Hannah, who desperately wanted a child but was barren for years. She poured out her heart in prayer, promising God that if He granted her a son, she would dedicate him to the Lord's service. Her heartfelt prayer in 1 Samuel 1:10-11 moved God's heart, and He answered her plea with the birth of Samuel. Hannah's story illustrates how prayer can carry burdens, express desires, and result in profound life changes.

In more contemporary times, Thomas, a man struggling with addiction, found that prayer was his turning point. After years of failed attempts to break free, he began to pray honestly and consistently, asking God for strength. Over time, he felt empowered to resist temptation and build a new life. Prayer became the cornerstone of his recovery journey, proving that when words are lifted honestly to God, lives can be transformed.

Prayer also serves as a compass when facing difficult decisions. The early church in Acts 13 prayed before sending out missionaries, seeking God's guidance and blessing. Today, many believers echo this practice. Sarah, a businesswoman in Australia, shares how prayer helped her navigate a challenging career change. Feeling uncertain, she prayed for clarity and peace. Over several months, through prayer and Scripture, she found confidence to start a nonprofit focused on helping women. Prayer didn't just provide answers; it shaped her heart to align with God's will.

Moreover, prayer fosters peace and resilience. Philippians 4:6-7 urges believers, *"Do not be anxious about anything, but in every situation, by prayer and petition, with thanksgiving, present your requests to God. And the peace of God, which transcends all understanding, will guard your hearts and your minds."*

This promise has encouraged many to turn to prayer in moments of stress, finding peace that surpasses human understanding.

The Bible also teaches that prayer is not just about asking but listening. Jesus often withdrew to quiet places to pray and listen to the Father's voice (Luke 5:16). This balance of speaking and listening deepens the relationship and opens believers to divine wisdom.

Prayer connects believers not only with God but with one another. Corporate prayer, as seen in Acts 4:31, unites hearts and multiplies spiritual power. Communities changed by prayer often report strengthened bonds and collective breakthroughs.

Finally, the transformative power of prayer lies in its ability to change the one who prays. As believers present their struggles, hopes, and gratitude to God, their perspectives shift, hearts soften, and faith grows. Prayer shapes character and aligns lives with God's purposes.

In a world full of noise and distractions, the Bible's teaching on prayer invites a return to stillness, trust, and connection with the divine. Through prayer, lives are changed—not just by what God does, but by what He does within the person who prays.

Chapter 14 – Living with Hope

Hope is a vital thread woven throughout the Bible, sustaining countless lives through hardship, uncertainty, and despair. Unlike wishful thinking or mere optimism, biblical hope is a confident expectation grounded in the character and promises of God. It lights the path forward, even when the future seems dark, and it empowers believers to endure and thrive.

The Bible's message of hope is clear in Romans 15:13: *"May the God of hope fill you with all joy and peace as you trust in him, so that you may overflow with hope by the power of the Holy Spirit."* This hope is not passive but active, overflowing into joy and peace as believers place their trust in God.

Consider the story of Joseph in the Old Testament, who was sold into slavery by his own brothers and wrongfully imprisoned. Despite these overwhelming setbacks, Joseph held onto hope in God's promises. Eventually, he rose to become second in command of Egypt, saving many lives during a famine. Joseph's story shows how hope anchored in God can carry a person through seemingly hopeless situations toward a victorious future.

In more recent history, Corrie Ten Boom's story—survivor of the Holocaust—shines as a beacon of hope. Amid unimaginable suffering, Corrie clung to biblical hope, trusting that God was present and purposeful. Her faith sustained her in the camps and later fueled her ministry of forgiveness and reconciliation, demonstrating that hope can flourish even in the darkest places.

Hope also transforms daily life and mental health. For Maria, a single mother struggling to provide for her children, biblical hope gave her strength to face each day with courage. She found encouragement in Jeremiah 29:11: *"For I know the plans I have for you," declares the Lord, "plans to prosper you and not to harm you, plans to give you a hope and a future."* This promise reshaped her perspective, turning anxiety into anticipation and exhaustion into perseverance.

Hope is a communal force as well. The early Christians, facing persecution and hardship, found in the resurrection of Jesus the ultimate source of hope—a hope that transcended death and promised eternal life. This hope sustained the church's growth and courage. Today, many believers in troubled regions around the world echo this ancient hope, finding strength to witness and serve despite opposition.

The Bible also teaches that hope is intertwined with faith and love (1 Corinthians 13:13). It is not a naive expectation but a steadfast trust in God's faithfulness. When hope is rooted in God, it resists despair and fuels perseverance. It empowers believers to look beyond present struggles to a future secured by God's promises.

Finally, living with hope means living with purpose and joy. Hope shapes how believers view suffering, setbacks, and challenges—not as the end but as part of a journey toward redemption and restoration. It creates resilience, inspires action, and spreads light to others who may be in darkness.

In a world often marked by uncertainty and fear, the Bible's call to hope changes lives by anchoring hearts to the unchanging God. This hope sustains, transforms, and propels believers forward, making life not only bearable but meaningful.

Chapter 15 – Serving Others

Serving others is a cornerstone of biblical teaching and one of the most practical ways the Bible changes lives. Far from being a burdensome duty, service rooted in Scripture transforms both the giver and the receiver, creating communities marked by compassion, justice, and love. The Bible teaches that true greatness is found not in status or wealth, but in humble service.

Jesus exemplified this truth throughout His ministry. In John 13, He famously washed His disciples' feet—a task considered menial and reserved for servants. He said, *"Now that I, your Lord and Teacher, have washed your feet, you also should wash one another's feet"* (John 13:14). This act underscored that serving others is not beneath anyone but is the very heart of Christian life.

Consider the story of Mother Teresa, who devoted her life to serving the poorest of the poor in Calcutta, India. Inspired by biblical teachings about caring for the "least of these" (Matthew 25:40), she saw service not as sacrifice alone but as an opportunity to reveal God's love. Her work transformed thousands of lives and inspired millions worldwide, showing how service flows from faith and changes the world.

Serving others also breaks down barriers of race, class, and culture. In Acts 6, the early church appointed deacons to ensure widows and needy members were cared for, illustrating that service strengthens community and fosters unity. Today, countless organizations rooted in Christian principles provide food, shelter, education, and medical care, embodying the Bible's call to love in action.

On a personal level, service often brings healing and purpose. Michael, a former gang member in the U.S., found new life when he began volunteering at a youth center. His past gave him unique insight and credibility, and through serving others, he experienced forgiveness and transformation. He says, "Serving others helped me find a reason to live and a way to give back what I once took."

The Bible also reminds believers that serving others is ultimately serving God. Colossians 3:23 says, *"Whatever you do, work at it with all your heart, as working for the Lord, not for human masters."* This perspective elevates everyday acts of kindness—from helping a neighbor to mentoring a child—into acts of worship and witness.

Serving others challenges selfishness and nurtures empathy. It opens hearts to the needs of the vulnerable and calls believers to live beyond themselves. The

Apostle Paul described love as *"patient and kind"* and *"always protects, always trusts, always hopes, always perseveres"* (1 Corinthians 13:4-7), qualities cultivated through service.

In communities where serving others becomes a lifestyle, social problems often decrease, relationships strengthen, and hope flourishes. The Bible's call to serve reshapes societies by promoting justice, mercy, and humility.

Ultimately, serving others changes lives because it reflects the nature of God Himself—a God who came not to be served but to serve (Mark 10:45). When believers embrace this calling, they not only impact the world but are themselves transformed into the image of Christ.

At the heart of the Bible's message is a call to serve. From Genesis to Revelation, God's people are commanded—and empowered—to care for others, putting their needs above our own. Serving is not just a duty; it is an act of love that reflects God's character and advances His kingdom.

Jesus set the ultimate example. The Son of God, who could have demanded honor and recognition, instead knelt to wash His disciples' feet (John 13:1–17). This act, considered one of the lowliest tasks in that culture, was not simply about cleanliness—it was a living illustration of humility, compassion, and selfless love. His words afterward remain a challenge to every believer: *"I have set you an example that you should do as I have done for you."*

Serving as a Reflection of Christ

Serving others is more than completing tasks or donating time; it is representing Christ to the world. When we serve in His name, our actions speak louder than our words. A warm meal for the hungry, a visit to the lonely, or a listening ear for the hurting all point people toward the God who cares for them.

The apostle Paul described this mindset in Philippians 2:3–4: *"Do nothing out of selfish ambition or vain conceit. Rather, in humility value others above yourselves, not looking to your own interests but each of you to the interests of the others."* This is the essence of Christlike service—voluntarily choosing to put another's well-being ahead of our own comfort.

The Joy of Serving

Many discover that serving others not only blesses those they help, but also brings deep personal joy and fulfillment. Jesus Himself said, *"It is more blessed to give than to receive"* (Acts 20:35). This blessing often comes in unexpected ways—through friendships formed, personal growth, or the quiet satisfaction of knowing you've been part of God's work in someone's life.

Rebecca, a young teacher, began volunteering at a homeless shelter because she "wanted to do something good." Over time, she realized the people she served were teaching her about gratitude, resilience, and faith in ways her comfortable life had never done. She says, "I went there to give, but I received far more than I ever expected."

Serving in Everyday Life

Not all service happens through organized programs or ministries. Much of it takes place in the ordinary flow of life—helping a neighbor with groceries, offering to babysit for a tired parent, or visiting someone in the hospital. These small, often unseen acts of kindness are just as valuable in God's eyes as large-scale projects.

Jesus taught that even giving "a cup of cold water" in His name will not go unrewarded (Matthew 10:42). This means no act of service is too small to matter. The key is the heart behind it—a willingness to love and give without expecting anything in return.

Serving in Times of Need

The Bible emphasizes serving especially in moments of crisis. The parable of the Good Samaritan (Luke 10:25–37) shows a man who went out of his way—and out of his comfort zone—to help someone in desperate need. His actions demonstrated that love is not defined by convenience, but by compassion.

During natural disasters, wars, or economic hardship, believers have a unique opportunity to embody Christ's love through practical help. Whether that's providing shelter, sharing resources, or simply being present with those who are grieving, such service becomes a living testimony of God's care.

Overcoming Barriers to Service

Some hesitate to serve because they feel unqualified, too busy, or unsure where to start. The Bible reminds us that God equips those He calls. The widow in 1 Kings 17 had only a handful of flour and a little oil, yet God used her to sustain the prophet Elijah—and in return, her own needs were met.

The call to serve is not limited to those with special training or abundant resources. It begins with a willing heart and a readiness to say, "Here am I, send me" (Isaiah 6:8).

A Real-Life Testimony: Mark's Journey to Service

Mark was a successful businessman whose life revolved around work, golf, and social events. Faith was something he kept at a polite distance. Then, after a serious health scare, he began attending church. One Sunday, he heard a sermon on John 13 and was struck by the image of Jesus washing feet. The pastor challenged the congregation to serve in a way that required humility.

Reluctantly, Mark signed up for a ministry that provided free car repairs for single mothers. The first Saturday, he spent hours in the hot sun fixing a worn-out brake system for a young woman named Tanya. When she burst into tears, saying she could now drive safely to her job, Mark felt a surge of joy unlike anything he'd known.

That day changed his priorities. He still runs his business, but now dedicates several weekends a month to serving others. "I thought I was too busy," Mark says, "but now I realize serving is the most important thing I do."

Closing Reflection

Serving others is not a burden but a privilege—a chance to join God in the work He is doing in the world. It shifts our focus from ourselves to the needs around us, reminding us that life is not about accumulating, but about giving. In the end, every act of service, whether seen or unseen, is an offering to God. As Jesus promised in Matthew 25:40, *"Whatever you did for one of the least of these brothers and sisters of mine, you did for me."*

Chapter 16 – The Transforming Power of Love

Love is the heartbeat of the Bible and the greatest force for transformation in human lives. The Bible reveals that God is love (1 John 4:8), and that His love is not only unconditional but also redemptive, powerful enough to change hearts, restore relationships, and inspire acts of selflessness. Through the Scriptures, people discover a love that redefines their identity and purpose.

The most profound example of God's love is found in the life and sacrifice of Jesus Christ. John 3:16 encapsulates this truth: *"For God so loved the world that he gave his one and only Son, that whoever believes in him shall not perish but have eternal life."* This divine love reaches beyond human limitations, offering forgiveness and new life to all who receive it.

Consider the story of Sarah, a woman who struggled with feelings of unworthiness and loneliness. Raised in a broken home and burdened by past mistakes, she believed she was unloved. But through reading Romans

8:38-39—which assures that nothing can separate us from God's love—Sarah experienced a profound internal shift. She realized that God's love was steadfast and personal. This discovery transformed her self-image, giving her the courage to pursue healthy relationships and serve others with compassion.

Love also transforms how people treat others. The Bible's call to *"love your neighbor as yourself"* (Matthew 22:39) challenges selfishness and nurtures empathy. In communities where biblical love takes root, violence diminishes, generosity increases, and social bonds strengthen.

An inspiring example comes from James and Ruth, a couple who started a ministry to help homeless youth in their city. Motivated by Christ's love, they provided shelter, counseling, and life skills training. Their work not only changed the lives of those they served but also deepened their own faith and sense of purpose.

The Bible also teaches that love is active and sacrificial. Paul's description of love in 1 Corinthians 13 portrays it as patient, kind, and enduring, capable of withstanding hardships. This love empowers believers to forgive offenses, serve sacrificially, and persevere in relationships.

Love's transformative power extends beyond individuals to entire societies. Movements for civil rights, humanitarian aid, and social justice have often been inspired and sustained by biblical love, demonstrating its capacity to reshape culture and promote dignity for all.

Furthermore, the Bible encourages believers to love even their enemies (Matthew 5:44), a revolutionary idea that breaks cycles of hatred and retaliation. This kind of love fosters reconciliation and peace, proving that transformation is possible even in the most broken situations.

Ultimately, the transforming power of love as revealed in the Bible changes lives by addressing the deepest human need—to be known, valued, and unconditionally loved. It heals wounds, inspires hope, and calls people to live lives marked by grace and compassion.

When people encounter the message of the Bible, one of the most profound changes they often experience is a new understanding of love—love that is not just a feeling, but a deliberate choice, a selfless action, and a guiding principle for life. The Bible does not merely speak about love in abstract terms; it defines it, models it, and invites people to practice it in everyday relationships.

The apostle Paul's famous words in **1 Corinthians 13** are not just poetic lines read at weddings—they are a radical blueprint for how love works in real life: *"Love is patient, love is kind. It does not envy, it does not boast, it is not proud."* This passage challenges people to move beyond natural impulses of selfishness, impatience, or irritation, and instead to embody a love that is patient, kind, and enduring.

For many, this transformation begins with realizing that they themselves are loved by God in an unconditional way. When someone truly believes that God loves them despite their past failures, insecurities, or shortcomings, it creates a deep sense of worth and security. This new identity often ripples outward, changing how they treat others. A person who once held grudges may now be quick to forgive. Someone who was distant or cold in relationships may begin to show warmth and compassion.

One woman named Claire shared that before she came to faith, she was a highly critical person—quick to point out flaws in others and slow to admit her own mistakes. Reading the Gospels opened her eyes to Jesus' mercy toward people who didn't deserve it. She said, "When I realized how much grace He gave me, I couldn't keep withholding it from others." Today, her family says she has gone from being "the harshest voice in the room" to "the most encouraging."

Love inspired by the Bible also transcends cultural barriers. In countries torn by ethnic division, believers often form friendships across lines that the wider society insists must remain divided. The Book of Acts tells how Jewish and Gentile followers of Jesus broke bread together, even though their cultures had been in conflict for generations. Modern-day examples abound: in places where racial or tribal tensions run high, churches become places where people from historically hostile groups worship side by side.

The Bible's love also shows itself in sacrificial service. In Matthew 25, Jesus describes love in action—not as warm feelings, but as feeding the hungry, clothing the needy, and visiting the sick and imprisoned. This teaching has inspired countless believers to volunteer in shelters, hospitals, and prisons—not for recognition, but because they see in each person the image of God.

A man named David once admitted he was obsessed with climbing the corporate ladder and rarely noticed the struggles of people around him. Then he read the parable of the Good Samaritan and realized he had been walking past "wounded travelers" every day—co-workers under stress, neighbors in need, even family members longing for his time. That conviction led him to reorient his life: he still works in business, but he now devotes evenings to mentoring at-risk teens.

The transforming power of love is one of the clearest pieces of evidence of the Bible's impact. It is not merely a set of rules or inspirational quotes—it is a call to live in a way that turns the world's definition of success upside down. In a culture that prizes self-promotion, the Bible calls people to humility. In a world that urges retaliation, it calls for forgiveness. In an age of isolation, it calls for community.

And the change is contagious. People who receive this kind of love often begin to extend it to others, creating a ripple effect. Families become more united, friendships grow deeper, communities become safer, and even enemies find common ground. This is why Jesus said in **John 13:35**, "By this everyone will know that you are my disciples, if you love one another."

The transformation may start small—an apology offered, a grudge released, a hand extended—but over time, these acts weave together into a life that reflects the heart of God. It is the kind of love that not only changes a person's life but can, in time, change the world.

Chapter 17 – Walking in Freedom

Freedom is a core theme in the Bible that profoundly impacts how people live and perceive themselves. The Bible teaches that true freedom is not merely the absence of external constraints but liberation from internal bondage—whether to sin, fear, guilt, or oppression. This spiritual freedom changes lives by releasing individuals to live authentically and purposefully.

Jesus declared in John 8:36, *"So if the Son sets you free, you will be free indeed."* This promise of freedom is both radical and personal. It breaks chains that no human power can undo and invites believers into a new way of living—a life marked by peace, joy, and moral clarity.

Consider the story of Carlos, who struggled for years with addiction and the feelings of shame and hopelessness it brought. Despite numerous attempts to quit, he felt trapped. It was only when he encountered the biblical message of freedom through Christ that he experienced true change. The truth that his identity was not defined by past mistakes but by God's grace empowered him to seek help, stay committed, and rebuild his life. Today, Carlos mentors' others, sharing how biblical freedom transformed him.

The Bible also highlights freedom from fear. Fear often controls decisions, relationships, and self-worth. But 2 Timothy 1:7 reminds believers that *"God gave us a spirit not of fear but of power and love and self-control."* This new spirit enables believers to face challenges boldly, free from paralyzing anxiety.

In a different context, Leah, a woman who grew up in an abusive environment, found freedom in the Bible's message. Through reading Psalm 34:18—*"The Lord is close to the brokenhearted and saves those who are crushed in spirit"*—and seeking support in a church community, she broke free from the cycle of fear and low self-esteem. The freedom she found shaped her healing journey and empowered her to advocate for others.

Biblical freedom also means freedom to live according to God's design, rather than being enslaved to harmful patterns or societal pressures. Paul writes in Galatians 5:1, *"It is for freedom that Christ has set us free. Stand firm, then, and do not let yourselves be burdened again by a yoke of slavery."* This calls believers to reject spiritual and moral slavery and embrace lives of integrity and purpose.

Freedom in the Bible is also linked to responsibility. It is not a license to do whatever one pleases but the liberty to choose what honors God and benefits others. This balance cultivates maturity, wisdom, and genuine peace.

Communities transformed by biblical freedom often become places of hope and renewal, where individuals support one another in living out their new identities. The freedom believers experience creates ripple effects that touch families, workplaces, and neighborhoods.

Ultimately, walking in freedom as taught by the Bible changes lives by liberating people from the invisible prisons of sin, shame, and fear. It invites them into a joyful, empowered existence rooted in God's love and truth.

Chapter 18 – Embracing Joy

Joy is a vibrant and transformative fruit of the Spirit, highlighted repeatedly throughout the Bible as more than fleeting happiness—a deep, abiding gladness rooted in God's presence and promises. Unlike temporary pleasures that fade, biblical joy sustains believers through trials, uplifts the weary, and reshapes outlooks, ultimately changing lives from the inside out.

The apostle Paul famously wrote in Philippians 4:4, *"Rejoice in the Lord always. I will say it again: Rejoice!"* This call to joy is remarkable, especially given Paul's own hardships, including imprisonment and persecution. His example demonstrates that joy is a choice grounded in faith rather than circumstances.

Take the Bible story of Esther, a young Jewish woman who became queen in a foreign land and faced the threat of genocide against her people. Despite the fear and uncertainty, her trust in God brought courage and a quiet joy that sustained her through difficult decisions. Her story reminds us that joy and hope often coexist with challenges.

In the modern world, Maria, a single mother working multiple jobs, found joy not in material wealth but in the biblical assurance that God's love was constant. Even amid exhaustion and financial stress, reading Psalm 16:11—*"You make known to me the path of life; you will fill me with joy in your presence"*—helped her maintain a joyful heart. This joy became contagious, influencing her children and community.

Joy also fuels resilience. During the civil rights movement, many leaders and participants drew strength from their faith, embracing joy as a source of hope and motivation amid oppression. The Bible's teaching that joy comes from God's salvation and presence empowered them to persevere for justice.

Moreover, joy deepens worship and community. The psalmists often celebrate joy as an expression of gratitude and reverence toward God. Joy-filled believers inspire and encourage one another, creating environments where faith thrives and lives are renewed.

The Bible also connects joy with obedience and gratitude. Jesus taught that abiding in His love produces joy (John 15:11), while Paul linked joy to thanksgiving and prayer (Philippians 4:6-7). This joyful living transforms mundane routines into opportunities for praise and thankfulness.

Importantly, biblical joy is not superficial or forced. It acknowledges pain and struggle but chooses to trust God's goodness beyond present circumstances. This perspective radically changes how people experience suffering and disappointment, turning trials into testimonies of hope.

In essence, embracing joy as taught in the Bible changes lives by filling hearts with peace, strengthening faith, and inspiring love. It offers a joyful defiance against despair and invites believers into a life marked by celebration of God's goodness.

Joy is often mistaken for mere happiness—a fleeting feeling tied to circumstances, possessions, or achievements. But the Bible reveals joy as something deeper, more enduring, and far more transformative. It is a fruit of the Spirit (Galatians 5:22), a sign of God's presence, and a strength that sustains believers even amid trials.

Jesus Himself spoke of joy repeatedly. In John 15:11, He said, *"I have told you this so that my joy may be in you and that your joy may be complete."* This joy is not dependent on life's ups and downs, but rooted in the unchanging truth of God's love and promises.

The Source of Biblical Joy

Biblical joy flows from a relationship with God. It begins with knowing that we are loved, accepted, and valued by the Creator of the universe. This knowledge creates a foundation that no external event can shake.

Consider the apostle Paul's life. Despite facing imprisonment, shipwrecks, and persecution, he wrote to the Philippians, *"Rejoice in the Lord always. I will say it again: Rejoice!"* (Philippians 4:4). Paul's joy was not a denial of suffering but a declaration that God's goodness transcends hardship.

Joy in the Midst of Trials

One of the most striking aspects of biblical joy is its presence during suffering. James 1:2–3 challenges believers to *"consider it pure joy… whenever you face trials of many kinds."* This does not mean delighting in pain itself, but recognizing that trials produce perseverance, maturity, and deeper faith.

A woman named Esther faced the heartache of losing her home and livelihood. Rather than sinking into despair, she found comfort in Psalm 16:11: *"You make known to me the path of life; you will fill me with joy in your presence."* Esther's joy came from trusting that God was leading her through the storm, even when the way was unclear.

Joy Through Worship and Gratitude

Joy is often cultivated through worship and thanksgiving. The Psalms overflow with calls to praise God, reminding believers that focusing on His character and faithfulness fuels joy.

During difficult seasons, intentionally choosing gratitude can reorient the heart. Instead of dwelling on what is lost or lacking, thanking God for His provision, presence, and promises opens the door for joy to grow.

Joy Shared with Others

Joy multiplies when shared. Christian community is a place where believers celebrate together, encouraging one another and bearing each other's burdens. The early church was known for its joy-filled fellowship, even amid persecution.

Acts 2:46–47 describes believers meeting daily with glad and sincere hearts, praising God and enjoying the favor of all the people. This joy was infectious, drawing others to the faith.

Joy as a Witness

In a world often marked by anxiety, sadness, and cynicism, joy stands out as a powerful testimony. People naturally want to know the source of a believer's inner peace and happiness. Joy rooted in faith reveals the hope and strength available through God.

A Real-Life Testimony: David's Joy Restored

David struggled with depression and loneliness after the loss of a close friend. For years, he felt like joy was out of reach. One day, a friend invited him to a church service focused on the story of Paul and Silas singing in prison (Acts 16:25).

David was struck by the image of worship and joy despite dire circumstances. He began reading the Bible and praying daily, asking God to restore his joy. Slowly, he noticed small moments of gratitude and hope returning. Today, David leads a support group where he shares his journey, encouraging others to find joy in God's presence, no matter the storms they face.

Closing Reflection

Joy is not a superficial emotion but a profound spiritual reality available to all who walk with God. It shines brightest in the darkest moments, reminding us that God's love, grace, and promises are steadfast. To embrace joy is to choose a perspective rooted in faith— a perspective that transforms not only our inner world but also the lives of those around us. As Nehemiah 8:10 says, *"The joy of the Lord is your strength."*

Chapter 19 – Growing in Wisdom

Wisdom is more than knowledge; it is the ability to live well—making choices that honor God, benefit others, and lead to a fulfilled life. The Bible presents wisdom as a precious gift, essential for navigating life's complexities and challenges. Growing in wisdom changes lives by transforming decisions, relationships, and character.

The book of Proverbs offers timeless wisdom, beginning with this profound declaration: *"The fear of the Lord is the beginning of wisdom"* (Proverbs 9:10). This fear is not terror but reverence—a deep respect for God that shapes how a person thinks and acts. Biblical wisdom starts with knowing God and trusting His guidance.

Consider Solomon, renowned for his God-given wisdom. When asked by God what he desired most, Solomon chose wisdom to govern his people well. His wise judgments, such as the famous story of the two women claiming the same baby (1 Kings 3), demonstrate the practical impact of biblical wisdom on justice and leadership.

In contemporary life, wisdom guides not only leaders but everyday people. Lisa, a young professional, found herself overwhelmed by career decisions and personal relationships. Through reading Proverbs and praying for wisdom (James 1:5 encourages believers to ask God for wisdom), she began making choices grounded in patience, integrity, and humility. This shift not only improved her career but also brought peace and stronger relationships.

Wisdom also guards against pitfalls. The Bible warns against pride, impulsiveness, and deceit—all destructive forces in life. Growing in wisdom involves self-awareness, learning from mistakes, and seeking counsel, as Proverbs 15:22 advises: *"Plans fail for lack of counsel, but with many advisers they succeed."* Communities that value biblical wisdom often see healthier families, better conflict resolution, and increased trust.

The story of Joseph in Egypt is another powerful example of wisdom in adversity. Sold into slavery, falsely accused, and imprisoned, Joseph did not lose hope. Instead, he applied wisdom and faith, interpreting dreams and managing resources that eventually saved nations from famine. His life illustrates how wisdom can turn hardship into opportunity.

Wisdom is also deeply relational. It fosters empathy, forgiveness, and kindness. James 3:17 describes wisdom that comes from heaven as *"first pure, then peace-loving, considerate, submissive, full of mercy and good fruit, impartial and sincere."* Such wisdom shapes how believers interact with others, building trust and harmony.

Finally, growing in wisdom is a lifelong journey. The Bible encourages continual learning and spiritual growth. As believers mature, they reflect God's character more clearly and navigate life with greater clarity and grace.

In a world full of confusing voices and competing values, biblical wisdom provides a steady guide. It changes lives by helping people live thoughtfully, justly, and lovingly—bringing glory to God and blessing to others.

Chapter 20 – Living a Life of Purpose

Living with purpose is a profound theme throughout the Bible, calling individuals to discover and embrace the unique reason God created them. The Bible teaches that every person has been made for meaningful work and that fulfilling this divine purpose leads to a life of joy, fulfillment, and impact. Understanding and living out God's purpose changes lives by giving direction, motivation, and hope.

The book of Jeremiah contains a powerful reminder of God's personal design for each life: *"For I know the plans I have for you," declares the Lord, "plans to prosper you and not to harm you, plans to give you a hope and a future"* (Jeremiah 29:11). This promise invites believers to trust that their lives matter deeply to God and that He desires good things for them.

Consider the story of Moses, who was called to lead the Israelites out of slavery despite his own doubts and fears. His purpose—to free and guide his people—gave him courage to face Pharaoh and endure hardships. Moses' life shows how embracing God's purpose can transform fear into boldness and uncertainty into confidence.

In modern times, Angela, a teacher in an underserved community, found her purpose through faith. Though the work was challenging and underappreciated, she saw her role as a calling to shape young lives. Inspired by Colossians 3:23—*"Whatever you do, work at it with all your heart, as working for the Lord"*—Angela's dedication brought hope and opportunity to her students, transforming her work into ministry.

Purpose also helps believers navigate setbacks and disappointments. The Apostle Paul endured imprisonment, rejection, and hardship, yet he remained focused on his mission to spread the Gospel. His writings reveal how purpose sustains perseverance and turns trials into testimony.

The Bible teaches that purpose is not just about grand achievements but everyday faithfulness. Small acts of kindness, service, and obedience contribute to God's larger plan. This perspective empowers believers to find meaning in all aspects of life, from parenting to professions to friendships.

Moreover, living a life of purpose aligns individuals with God's will, creating harmony and peace. Ephesians 2:10 says, *"For we are God's handiwork, created in Christ Jesus to do good works, which God prepared in advance for us to do."* This verse emphasizes that purpose is part of God's design and plan.

Living with purpose also impacts communities and future generations. Purpose-driven lives inspire others, build strong families, and foster thriving communities. When believers embrace their God-given purpose, their lives become testimonies that draw others toward hope and faith.

Ultimately, living a life of purpose as taught by the Bible changes lives by giving them meaning, direction, and fulfillment. It invites every person into a vibrant relationship with God that empowers them to make a lasting difference in the world.

Chapter 21 – More Actual Examples of Changed Lives

Throughout history and across cultures, countless individuals testify to the life-changing impact of the Bible. These stories—diverse in background, age, and circumstance—demonstrate how the Scriptures inspire transformation, hope, and renewed purpose in ways that are tangible and lasting.

One well-known example, that was already mentioned, is John Newton, a former slave trader who experienced a dramatic conversion after reading the Bible. Once involved in a cruel and immoral trade, Newton's encounter with Scripture led him to repentance and a new life dedicated to faith and abolitionism. He went on to write the beloved hymn *Amazing Grace*, a timeless testimony of redemption and God's mercy.

In contemporary times, consider Tony Campolo, a sociologist and speaker whose early life was marked by struggles with faith and doubt. A close study of the Bible helped him find clarity, purpose, and a passion for social justice that shaped his career and ministry, influencing thousands.

There are countless stories from everyday people whose lives have been changed by the Bible's message. Maria, a woman battling addiction, found freedom through Scripture's promise of forgiveness and new beginnings. Her journey from despair to hope illustrates the Bible's power to restore dignity and purpose.

Mark, a man estranged from his family, found reconciliation after embracing biblical teachings on forgiveness and love. The Bible helped him break down walls of bitterness and rebuild relationships that once seemed lost.

The Bible has also transformed communities. In places torn by violence or poverty, groups inspired by Scripture have initiated healing ministries, education programs, and social justice efforts. These collective transformations show the Bible's power beyond individual lives, impacting society for good.

Even skeptics and critics have testified to the Bible's influence. Some began with doubts but found its wisdom and moral vision compelling enough to alter their worldview and lifestyle.

The common thread in all these stories is that the Bible meets people in their reality—with its challenges, hopes, and failures—and invites them into transformation. It offers not just rules but grace, not just commands but encouragement.

These real-life examples highlight that the Bible's power to change lives is not confined to a certain time or place. It continues to work dynamically in hearts and communities, proving itself relevant and alive.

The Bible changes lives through its message of love, redemption, and hope—empowering people to overcome adversity, build meaningful relationships, and live with purpose. These stories serve as a testament to that enduring truth, inviting readers to explore how their own lives might be changed through engagement with Scripture.

Chapter 22 - Practical Steps for Real Change

The Bible is not meant to be admired from a distance like an ancient artifact in a museum. It is God's living Word, active and relevant today, designed to transform our thinking, guide our decisions, and shape our character in real and tangible ways. Many people sincerely believe in the Bible but find themselves struggling when it comes to actually living it out. A dusty Bible on a shelf cannot change a life, and even reading Scripture without putting it into practice will leave our hearts largely untouched. The true power of God's Word is released when it moves from the page to the heart, and from the heart into our words, choices, and daily actions.

The first step toward living the Bible daily is reading it with purpose, not merely as part of a rushed routine. Too often we read Scripture the way we skim through a newspaper, looking for a few interesting lines before moving on with our day. Instead, we must approach the Bible with focused intention. This means setting aside a consistent time when distractions are minimal—whether it's in the quiet of the morning, the calm of the evening, or during a lunch break at work. Choosing a reading plan that fits your season of life is also vital. Some may thrive on reading a chapter a day; others may prefer a chronological plan that traces the Bible's story from Genesis to Revelation; still others may want to linger in a single book for a month, diving deep into its message. Above all, each reading should begin with prayer, asking God to open our eyes to the truths He wants us to see. As Psalm 119:18 says, "Open my eyes that I may see wonderful things in your law."

As we read, it is important to engage with Scripture actively rather than passively. This can be done by taking notes, underlining key phrases, and writing down verses that stand out. Asking thoughtful questions—"What does this reveal about God? What does it teach me about human nature? What does it expose in my own life?"— helps us move from reading words to hearing God speak. We should also pay attention to repeated words or themes, because repetition often signals a truth that God wants to emphasize. By approaching the Bible like an eager student, we turn it from a book we "get through" into a personal conversation with the Author.

Living out the Bible's teaching becomes more manageable when we focus on applying one truth at a time. Trying to overhaul our entire life in one week is often overwhelming and unsustainable. Instead, after reading, we can choose one truth or command to put into practice that very day. If we read about patience, for example, we might consciously decide to remain calm during a frustrating moment that would normally trigger irritation. Recording the experience in a small notebook or phone app helps reinforce the lesson and track our growth. These small, specific acts of obedience may seem simple, but over time they shape our character and bring lasting change.

Memorizing key verses is another powerful way to make the Bible part of daily life. When we commit Scripture to memory, it becomes a ready tool for moments of temptation, fear, or important decisions. Choosing a verse that speaks directly to a personal struggle or goal—such as anxiety, forgiveness, or perseverance—ensures that it will be relevant and immediately useful. Repeating it aloud in the morning, at midday, and before bed, and placing it somewhere visible like a bathroom mirror or phone lock screen, helps engrain it into our thoughts. This was the very strategy Jesus Himself used in the wilderness, responding to temptation with "It is written" (Matthew 4). If this approach was effective for Him, it should be central to our own spiritual defense.

The process of living the Bible also involves sharing what we learn with others. Speaking about Scripture often deepens our own understanding and strengthens our commitment to live it out. This could mean discussing a verse with a friend, sharing a brief insight during a family meal, or participating in a Bible study group. Even posting a short reflection online can spark conversation and encourage someone else. When we speak God's Word, it not only blesses others but reinforces the truth in our own hearts.

Applying the Bible daily also means letting it influence both the small and large decisions of life. The Bible is not limited to "spiritual" topics like prayer or worship—it addresses relationships, finances, work ethics, forgiveness, and even how we respond to stress. When faced with a choice, we can ask, "Does the Bible speak directly to this?" or "What principle from Scripture can guide me here?" The more often we bring the Bible into our decision-making, the more naturally we will think and act from a biblical perspective rather than reacting from emotion or habit.

Finally, it is helpful to pause every few months and evaluate our progress. Are we reading the Bible regularly? Are we applying what we learn in practical ways? Are others noticing changes in our speech, attitudes, or actions? Honest reflection, combined with prayer, keeps us on track. The goal is not perfection but steady progress in becoming more like Christ.

James 1:22 warns, "Do not merely listen to the word, and so deceive yourselves. Do what it says." The Bible has the power to reshape our lives, but it calls for our active participation. Each time we read, remember, and act on God's Word, we take another step forward in the lifelong journey of transformation. A life shaped by Scripture does not happen overnight, but with steady, intentional practice, the Bible becomes more than a book we read—it becomes the lens through which we see the world and the foundation upon which we build every part of life.

Chapter 23 – Those Who Tried to Disprove the Bible

It is a curious fact of history that some of the Bible's most devoted defenders started as its fiercest critics. These individuals were not casual doubters—they were scholars, lawyers, journalists, detectives, scientists, and everyday men and women who set out with the deliberate aim of dismantling the Christian faith. Some were motivated by academic pride, others by personal resentment, and still others by a desire to "rescue" loved ones from what they viewed as superstition.

But in each case, the deeper they dug, the more the Bible stood unshaken. The ancient texts withstood the blows of their skepticism. Instead of crumbling, they shone more brightly under scrutiny, forcing these skeptics to confront the possibility that they were wrong—not just intellectually, but about the very purpose of life. The following stories are powerful reminders that truth fears no investigation, and that the Bible does not require blind faith; it invites honest examination.

Sir William Ramsay – The Archaeologist Who Couldn't Deny the Evidence

In the late 1800s, Sir William Ramsay's reputation as an archaeologist was unmatched. Educated at Oxford and trained under leading German scholars, he was firmly convinced that much of the New Testament was a fabrication written long after the events it described. His professors had assured him that the book of Acts, in particular, was riddled with historical inaccuracies— mere pious fiction.

Determined to prove it, Ramsay set off on a series of expeditions to Asia Minor, traveling by horseback and on foot through the rugged landscapes mentioned in Acts. He traced the missionary journeys of the Apostle Paul, expecting to find a trail of historical blunders.

Instead, something remarkable happened. Everywhere Ramsay went, Luke's meticulous details checked out. Political titles matched exactly with archaeological inscriptions from the era. Town names, once thought to be fictional, were confirmed to have existed precisely as Luke described. Even small geographic notes—like the placement of certain cities in relation to rivers and mountains—were proven accurate.

By the end of his journey, Ramsay's skepticism had collapsed. The book he expected to discredit had won his admiration as a model of historical precision. Ramsay not only became a Christian but wrote extensively defending the reliability of Scripture, calling Luke "a historian of the first rank." The man who set out to bury Acts instead became one of its greatest advocates.

C. S. Lewis – The Reluctant Convert

Clive Staples Lewis, known to the world as C. S. Lewis, was not always the warm, imaginative Christian writer we remember. As a young man, he was a committed atheist. The horrors of World War I, which he experienced firsthand as a soldier, had hardened him. The death of his mother in his youth had left him bitter toward any idea of a loving God.

At Oxford University, Lewis immersed himself in literature and philosophy, surrounding himself with brilliant thinkers who shared his skepticism. He dismissed Christianity as one myth among many, no more credible than the stories of Zeus or Odin. Yet he loved myth and beauty, and somewhere deep inside, he longed for something more than cold rationalism.

His turning point began quietly—with conversations. Fellow professors like Hugo Dyson and his close friend J. R. R. Tolkien challenged his assumptions, pointing out that Christianity was unique among myths: it claimed to be history. If Jesus truly lived, died, and rose again, then the story was not merely a tale—it was the truth.

Late one night, Lewis walked and talked with Tolkien until the early hours. They spoke of ancient myths, the longing of the human heart, and the possibility that all myths were shadows of a greater reality fulfilled in Christ. Within weeks, Lewis found himself reluctantly believing that God was real. Later, while riding in the sidecar of his brother's motorcycle to the zoo, he crossed the line from theism to Christianity, without fireworks or visions—just a quiet, steady certainty.

Lewis called himself "the most dejected and reluctant convert in all England," but his surrender to Christ changed the course of his life. The skeptic became one of the most persuasive Christian apologists of the 20th century.

Lee Strobel – The Journalist on a Mission

Lee Strobel's skepticism was more personal. As the legal editor of the *Chicago Tribune*, Strobel had spent his career demanding evidence. Facts were sacred; faith, to him, was wishful thinking.

When his wife, Leslie, became a Christian, he was alarmed. He feared her new beliefs would create distance in their marriage. Determined to save her from what he saw as a dangerous delusion; he embarked on a personal investigation—using every tool of journalism and legal reasoning at his disposal.

For nearly two years, Strobel interviewed leading scholars in history, archaeology, and textual criticism. He examined ancient manuscripts, weighed medical evidence for the crucifixion, and studied the testimony of early Christian witnesses. The central claim of Christianity—the resurrection—stood at the heart of his investigation. If Jesus had not risen from the dead,

Christianity was a sham. If He had, the implications were undeniable.

In the end, Strobel found the evidence too compelling to ignore. The historical reliability of the Gospels, the early dating of the accounts, and the explosive growth of the early church all pointed to one conclusion: Jesus truly rose. Strobel gave his life to Christ and wrote *The Case for Christ*, a book that has since reached millions of readers and sparked countless other journeys from doubt to faith.

Frank Morrison – The Lawyer Who Changed His Case

Frank Morrison was an English journalist and lawyer who prided himself on his rational thinking. Like Strobel, he saw Christianity's claims about the resurrection as weak and unconvincing. Convinced that a legal analysis would expose it, he began writing a book to refute it.

But as Morrison examined the Gospel accounts with the precision of a courtroom attorney, his skepticism began to crumble. The accounts were too early to be legend, too consistent in their core details, and too costly for the witnesses to have invented. The disciples had nothing to gain—and everything to lose—by proclaiming a risen Christ, yet they did so boldly, even unto death.

The evidence forced Morrison to an unexpected verdict: Jesus had indeed risen from the dead. The book he had intended to write against Christianity became *Who*

Moved the Stone? a powerful defense of the resurrection that continues to influence seekers today.

Modern-Day Examples of Skeptics Turned Believers

While the stories of famous skeptics-turned-believers are inspiring, they can feel distant to the average person. What about those who don't have advanced degrees or global platforms? In living rooms, coffee shops, workplaces, and even internet chat rooms, ordinary people have also set out to challenge the Bible—only to be changed by it. These accounts prove that God meets both the scholar and the everyman with the same life-altering truth.

The Police Detective from California

Mark was a veteran homicide detective. He'd worked dozens of murder cases and prided himself on his ability to spot lies. Raised without religion, he viewed the Bible as a collection of myths for the gullible. One day, a friend challenged him: "Why not examine the Gospels like you would a cold case file?"

Mark approached the task with the same rigor he used at work. He analyzed the eyewitness accounts of Jesus' life, paying close attention to the differences in perspective, the specific details, and the apparent absence of collusion among the writers. Instead of finding contradictions, he found patterns consistent with genuine eyewitness testimony.

Mark became convinced that the resurrection was the

best explanation for the evidence. His investigation led him to Christ, and today he mentors young officers, telling them, "Truth doesn't fear the badge—or the Bible."

The Scientist in the Lab

Angela was a microbiologist working in a university research lab. She considered herself "spiritual but not religious" and had little patience for what she saw as the anti-scientific claims of the Bible. Her turning point came when she joined an online discussion forum to "set Christians straight" about evolution and the origins of life.

In preparing her arguments, Angela began reading both the Bible and books by Christian scientists. She was startled to find that the Bible wasn't in conflict with the scientific method but often invited curiosity, urging readers to "test all things" (1 Thessalonians 5:21). She wrestled for months with the idea that the same God who created the laws of nature could also perform miracles within   them.
Her final surrender came after reading John's Gospel and realizing that faith in Christ was not blind acceptance but a reasoned trust in the One who claimed, "I am the truth." Angela was baptized a year later.

The Former Online Atheist Blogger

James ran a popular blog dedicated to "debunking" Christianity. He mocked Bible verses, highlighted Old Testament laws he found absurd, and encouraged readers to reject faith entirely. One day, a Christian professor began respectfully responding to his posts—not with insults, but with historical and textual evidence James had never encountered.

Intrigued, James began privately corresponding with the professor. Over months of dialogue, James realized that many of his criticisms were based on strawman versions of Christianity rather than what the Bible actually taught. Reading the Gospels for himself, he encountered the person of Jesus in a way that dismantled his hostility. James shut down his blog, explaining in his final post that "the man I once mocked is now the Lord I worship."

The Woman in the Hospital Waiting Room

Carla was sitting in a hospital waiting room when she overheard two nurses discussing their Bible study. Annoyed, she later told them, "You're wasting your time—science has disproven the Bible." Instead of arguing, the nurses invited her to their next meeting. Out of curiosity (and perhaps a little pride), Carla went, intending to point out flaws in their discussion.

But as the weeks went on, Carla found herself drawn to the humility and joy she saw in the group. The Scriptures they read didn't just speak of ancient events; they spoke to her personal struggles, fears, and hopes. One night, while reading Psalm 34:18—*"The Lord is close to the brokenhearted and saves those who are crushed in spirit"*—Carla realized she was the one who needed saving.

A Pattern Across All Stories

Whether in an Oxford lecture hall or a police precinct, in a journalist's newsroom or a hospital waiting room, these stories share a common theme: the Bible is not afraid of honest scrutiny. These people approached Scripture with suspicion, even hostility. But in confronting the text, they found not just historical credibility or logical consistency—they found the living Christ.

The transformation from skeptic to believer is not about losing the ability to question; it's about discovering that the ultimate answers lie in the God who welcomes questions and then calls us to follow Him.

Chapter 24 - Helping Others Experience the Bible's Power

Transformation through the Bible is never meant to be a solitary journey. When God changes our lives, He invites us to become instruments of that same change in others. Passing the torch—sharing the life-giving message of Scripture—is both a privilege and a responsibility for every believer. But for many, the idea of talking about faith feels intimidating or overwhelming. How do we begin? What if we don't have all the answers? The good news is that helping others experience the Bible's power often begins with something simple and deeply personal: sharing your own story. Your testimony—the honest recounting of how God's Word impacted your life—holds a unique power that no argument or debate can match. It breaks down walls, opens hearts, and offers a tangible example of what faith looks like in the real world.

In everyday life, opportunities to introduce the Bible's message often arise naturally—in conversations with friends, family, coworkers, or even strangers. It's important to approach these moments with humility and genuine care rather than pressure or judgment. Listening attentively to others' struggles and hopes can create openings to share a meaningful verse or a brief insight that brought you comfort or clarity. Sometimes, simply offering to pray for someone or inviting them to join a small Bible study can plant seeds of curiosity and hope. These small gestures, when done sincerely, demonstrate the practical relevance of Scripture without overwhelming the other person.

Countless modern examples show how faith spreads when believers invest time and love in mentoring or small-group settings. One-on-one relationships allow for deeper questions, honest doubts, and gradual growth. Small groups create safe environments where people feel supported as they explore Scripture together. Those who have experienced transformation often find that guiding others strengthens their own faith, deepens their understanding of the Bible, and enriches their spiritual journey. The joy of watching someone take their first steps toward God or witnessing their life change because of the Word is a powerful motivation to keep sharing.

Remember, you don't have to be a Bible scholar or have perfect words to make a difference. Sometimes the simplest acts—giving a friend a copy of a favorite verse, inviting a neighbor to church, or sharing a personal story of hope—are the most effective ways to pass on the torch. God works through willing hearts and open hands. He multiplies faith not because of our eloquence, but because of His power working through us.

Passing the torch is also an ongoing journey. It requires patience, prayer, and persistence. Not everyone will respond immediately, and some may reject the message altogether. Yet, the Bible assures us that the seeds we plant are never wasted. Like the farmer who patiently waits for the harvest, we trust God to bring growth in His timing.

Ultimately, helping others experience the Bible's power is not only about changing their lives—it also deepens our own transformation. As we teach, encourage, and support, we reflect God's love more clearly. The cycle of grace continues, and the light of Scripture spreads further with each new heart it touches.

In passing the torch, we become part of a greater story—a story that began thousands of years ago and continues today, inviting every generation to know, live, and share the life-changing truth of God's Word.

Chapter 25 – Conclusions

The journey through the pages of this book has explored how the Bible changes lives in profound and multifaceted ways. From building moral foundations to embracing joy, from walking in freedom to living with purpose, the Bible offers timeless truths that touch every aspect of human existence. These truths are not abstract ideas but living principles that have transformed individuals, families, communities, and nations throughout history and continue to do so today.

One of the most striking conclusions is that the Bible's impact is deeply personal yet universally relevant. Whether someone is seeking peace in troubled times, strength through faith, or the courage to forgive, the Bible meets them where they are and offers hope. Its message transcends culture, language, and era, revealing a God who loves, redeems, and restores.

Another key takeaway is the Bible's invitation to relationship. More than a rulebook or history, the Bible is a guide to knowing and walking with God. It encourages trust, obedience, and openness to transformation. As readers engage with its words, they discover that change begins not with external circumstances but with the heart.

Throughout the chapters, stories of real people—ancient and modern—illustrate how biblical principles work in daily life. These stories remind us that transformation is possible regardless of background, mistakes, or hardships. The Bible's power lies in its ability to offer grace alongside truth, encouraging growth without condemnation.

The themes of love, faith, hope, and service emerge as central to this transformation. They are not merely ideals but practical forces that shape decisions, relationships, and character. As these qualities take root, lives are healed, communities are strengthened, and purpose is found.

Importantly, the Bible acknowledges the complexity of life. It does not promise a life free from challenges but offers tools to face them with courage and peace. Its message of redemption assures that failures do not have the final word and that renewal is always possible.

As readers close this book, the hope is that they will carry forward the lessons and inspirations found within its chapters. The Bible's power to change lives is ongoing, accessible to anyone who seeks it with an open heart. It calls each person to a journey of discovery, growth, and abundant life.

In conclusion, the Bible remains a transformative force in a changing world—a source of wisdom, comfort, and hope that continues to shape lives in ways both profound and practical. Engaging with the Bible is not just an intellectual exercise but an invitation to experience the life-changing love and grace of God.

Additional Reading Choices

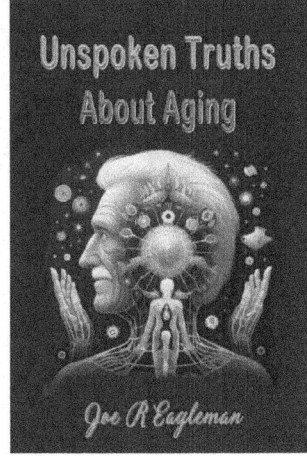

ABOUT THE AUTHOR

Joe R. Eagleman (1936-) was born on a farm near West Plains Missouri. He received the PhD from the University of Missouri in 1963 and was a professor at the University of Kansas for 39 years. He taught thousands of students about Atmospheric Science through his courses there and many thousands more  through four different textbooks used by over a hundred universities over a span of several decades. He directed a successful experiment on Skylab, funded by NASA, and invented a tornado in his laboratory that was used by Universal Studios for a 50 ft. tornado attraction in the Twister Building in Orlando Florida for several decades. It can still be seen at the Exploratorium in San Francisco.

He is the author of a technical book on severe thunderstorms that includes his tornado safety research which resulted in changes that were adopted nationally. His autobiography, *Name Your Price*, tells of his early life on a farm where he was the 11th of 12 children. It includes his work as a scientist as well as a number of unusual hobbies including those as an artist, musician, luthier, marksman, taxidermist, world traveler and other endeavors.

He has also published his second autobiography, *Monumental Moments,* that captures the most significant times of his life and *Eagleman Stories* that contains stories from his life as well as his 11 siblings and his parents.

Since his retirement he has published numerous books and recorded four albums of original music. For more information see http://www.JoeEagleman.com.